EVOLVE

WORKBOOK

Carolyn Clarke Flores and Michele Lewis

5

T0306674

CAMBRIDGE
UNIVERSITY PRESS

CAMBRIDGE
UNIVERSITY PRESS & ASSESSMENT

Shaftesbury Road, Cambridge CB2 8EA, United Kingdom

One Liberty Plaza, 20th Floor, New York, NY 10006, USA

477 Williamstown Road, Port Melbourne, VIC 3207, Australia

314–321, 3rd Floor, Plot 3, Splendor Forum, Jasola District Centre, New Delhi – 110025, India

103 Penang Road, #05–06/07, Visioncrest Commercial, Singapore 238467

Cambridge University Press & Assessment is a department of the University of Cambridge.

We share the University's mission to contribute to society through the pursuit of education, learning and research at the highest international levels of excellence.

www.cambridge.org
Information on this title: www.cambridge.org/9781108409070

First published 2020

20 19 18 17 16 15 14 13 12 11 10 9 8 7 6 5

Printed in Malaysia by Vivar Printing

A catalogue record for this publication is available from the British Library

ISBN 9781108405331 Student's Book
ISBN 9781108405119 Student's Book A
ISBN 9781108409261 Student's Book B
ISBN 9781108405348 Student's Book with Practice Extra
ISBN 9781108405133 Student's Book with Practice Extra A
ISBN 9781108409278 Student's Book with Practice Extra B
ISBN 9781108409070 Workbook with Audio
ISBN 9781108408813 Workbook with Audio A
ISBN 9781108411950 Workbook with Audio B
ISBN 9781108405195 Teacher's Edition with Test Generator
ISBN 9781108410748 Presentation Plus
ISBN 9781108412056 Class Audio CDs
ISBN 9781108408004 Video Resource Book with DVD
ISBN 9781108414500 Full Contact with DVD
ISBN 9781108411561 Full Contact with DVD A
ISBN 9781108414210 Full Contact with DVD B
Additional resources for this publication at www.cambridge.org/evolve

CONTENTS

UNIT 1 STEP FORWARD

1.1 LIFE CHANGES

1 VOCABULARY: Facing challenges

A **Complete the sentences with the words in the box.**

accept	adapt	resist	survive	tackle	~~underestimate~~	welcome

1 Law school students often *underestimate* the amount of homework they will get. It is usually more than they expected.

2 Marisol finally decided to ______ graduate school. She plans to start next year.

3 She didn't take the job because she couldn't ______ the low salary.

4 When Daniel moved from Boston to Phoenix, it took him a few months to ______ to the hot climate.

5 I did not think I would ______ my first year as a doctor because it was so difficult. Luckily, kind coworkers helped me get through it.

6 If you ______ making changes in your life, you won't grow or have new experiences.

7 My boss told me I was ______ to participate in the meeting.

B **Match the challenges with the correct solution.**

1 You can't take crowds. *e*
2 You're capable of managing people. ___
3 You underestimated the amount of time you needed. ___
4 You're frightened of getting lost. ___
5 You got through medical school. ___
6 You want to take a step forward in your career. ___
7 You can't get a grip on Spanish. ___
8 You can't cope with studying for a higher degree. ___

a Study in Mexico.
b Use a good map.
c Don't go to graduate school.
d Look for training opportunities.
e Don't move to a big city.
f You expect to earn a good salary.
g You'll be a good boss.
h Schedule more time for the task.

2 GRAMMAR: Present habits

A **Circle the correct answer to complete each sentence.**

1 Ivan ___ friends easily. He'll meet a lot of new people when he moves.
- a tends to making
- (b) tends to make
- c is making

2 When I'm looking for a new job, ___ to as many companies as possible.
- a I'm applying
- b I applied
- c I apply

3 I ___ trying to learn new skills. I think that's the key to success.

a am constantly

b tend to

c constantly

4 When I take a difficult class, I ___ my professor for help at least once a week.

a am asking

b always asking

c ask

5 I ___ for different ways to stay healthy. Yesterday, I went to a new exercise class.

a always look

b always looking

c am always look

6 When ___ bored with my classes, I think about changing my major.

a feel

b I'm feeling

c I'm feel

B **Complete the sentences using the correct form of the verbs in parentheses.**

1 I'm always *wondering* what my life will be like when I *retire*. (wonder, retire)

2 When she's ___ stressed, she usually ___ her friend Stephan for support. (feel, call)

3 He tends to ___ more after he ___ a new exercise routine. (eat, start)

4 I often ___ about changing my career to something completely different. (think)

5 He's always ___ his friends that they should travel if they ever ___ the chance. (tell, get)

6 I tend to ___ very excited for people when they ___ they're getting married. (get, announce)

7 He's always ___ for new opportunities to make money and will ___ all of his friends to support him. (look, ask)

3 GRAMMAR AND VOCABULARY

A **Complete the sentences so that they are true for you.**

1 I tend to resist *trying new kinds of food*.

2 I usually underestimate ___.

3 I'm feeling encouraged by ___.

4 I survive difficult times by ___.

5 I'm always adapting to ___.

6 I tend to accept ___.

B **Write three more sentences with information that is true for you. Use *tend to*, *will*, and the present continuous.**

___

___

___

___

___

1.2 MEMORY LANE

1 VOCABULARY: Describing annoying things

A **Choose the correct words or phrases to complete each sentence.**

1 I always feel ______ when I give a presentation. I don't like to speak in public.
  (a) awkward b frustrating
2 I study Arabic and I think the grammar is ______ . I don't fully understand it yet.
  a a waste of time b complex
3 It takes time to find a new job, so don't ______ . Just take a break, and then try again.
  a lose patience b get on your nerves
4 Can you please stop whistling? It's starting to ______ .
  a drive you crazy b get on my nerves
5 To me, nothing is more ______ than when coworkers are late for a meeting.
  a time-consuming b infuriating
6 I used to think school was ______ . When I got older, I realized how valuable it had been.
  a a waste of time b clumsy
7 The early days of the internet were ______ because it took a long time to connect to websites, and then the connection was frequently lost.
  a frustrating b hard to operate
8 Writing a research paper is so ______ . I wish I could write more quickly.
  a tricky b time-consuming
9 I remember my first cell phone. It was ______ until I learned how it worked. Then, it was very easy.
  a time-consuming b hard to operate
10 Understanding modern technology can be ______ , especially for people from older generations who didn't grow up with it.
  a tricky b hard to operate

2 GRAMMAR: Past habits

A **Correct the mistakes in each sentence. There may be more than one way to correct each mistake.**

1 When I got sick, my grandmother would ~~made~~ make me chicken soup.
2 Before texting, we don't use to be in touch with our friends so often.
3 I would ate soup every day until I felt better.
4 I used to love go to the video store to rent movies.
5 My parents didn't used to let me watch a lot of television.
6 We used to played cards and board games instead.
7 I never use to like playing video games.
8 I am used to read books on rainy days.

B **Change the sentences to show past habits. Use *(not/never) used to* or *would (not)*. There may be more than one answer.**

1 They exchanged gifts on the holidays.
They would exchange gifts on the holidays.

2 She cuts her daughter's hair.

3 He took a lot of photographs.

4 We don't play video games.

5 I picked them up from school.

6 You never study for your exams.

3 GRAMMAR AND VOCABULARY

A **Imagine you grew up in a time without the inventions in the box below. Write sentences about your past habits before these inventions. Use (*not/never*) *used to*, or *would* (*not*) and the vocabulary from exercise 1A.**

cars electricity eye glasses internet ~~smartphones~~ washing machines

1 It used to be frustrating to travel to new cities before smartphones were invented because I would often get lost.

2

3

4

5

6

1.3 UPGRADE

1 LISTENING

A 1.01 **Listen to the conversation and circle the correct answer.**

1 According to Professor Silva, what is confusing for the students?
  - **a** how they survived without smartphones in the past
  - **b** the different rules on smartphones in class
  - **c** why they have to have discussions with each other in class

2 What does Professor Novak think about smartphones in class?
  - **a** She uses them too much.
  - **b** They're useful in a lot of ways.
  - **c** They shouldn't be allowed.

3 By the end of the conversation, both professors:
  - **a** lose their patience.
  - **b** disagree with each other.
  - **c** agree that cell phones can help students.

2 CRITICAL THINKING

A THINK CRITICALLY **What are the advantages and disadvantages of using a smartphone in a language class? How could it help you with reading, pronunciation, and listening?**

3 SPEAKING

A **Put the conversation in order.**

___ **A** Yeah, standing in line for tickets and popcorn was part of the excitement. Generally speaking, movies aren't as much fun now. Sure, you can watch from home, but you have to watch it alone or with only a few friends. It was better watching a great movie with a big crowd of people.

___ **B** Count me in! As for *Star Wars*, I have a costume for almost every character. I'll be there.

1 **A** It's so easy to watch movies nowadays, but I really miss going to the theater.

___ **A** When it comes to wearing costumes, I usually have a costume party every time a new *Star Wars* movie comes out. You should come next time. It'll be a lot of fun.

___ **B** That is so true! Remember when the first *Harry Potter* movie came out? There were so many people there. Everyone wore costumes of their favorite characters. It was like a big party.

___ **B** I couldn't agree more. I miss it, too. Overall, watching movies is easy nowadays, but it's also boring. I used to love standing in line to get tickets, buy popcorn …

B **Choose one of the topics. Write a conversation between two people. Use phrases for discussing issues and agreeing strongly.**

1 People are healthier now than they used to be.
2 We used to communicate with each other more frequently.
3 Classroom teaching has improved because of technology.
4 Social media is a waste of time.

A ______________________________

B ______________________________

A ______________________________

B ______________________________

A ______________________________

B ______________________________

1.4 BACK TO BASICS

1 READING

A **IDENTIFY MAIN IDEAS** **What types of activities could tourists do on a farm? Make a list and then read the text to check your answers.**

TAKING TOURISM BACK TO ITS ROOTS

Home News About

These days, it often seems like computers do everything for us. But even with all the progress that technology has made, there is comfort in the traditional ways of life. That's why agritourism is on the rise and should continue to be promoted.

Agritourism refers to activities for tourists that take place on a farm or a ranch. There are two main goals of agritourism: to provide meaningful experiences for tourists and to help the farm industry stay alive. The farming economy has suffered. The cost of farm equipment has increased and younger generations don't want to cope with the difficult life of farming, so there is no one to carry on the work.

However, agritourism, which is a branch of eco-tourism, is now a fast-growing part of the travel and tourism economy, and is helping the farm industry improve.

Perhaps you've taken part in this style of tourism without knowing it. Many experiences count as agritourism, such as touring a ranch or visiting a vineyard. Maybe you've visited a farm and collected fresh eggs, or learned to perform some of the many farming tasks that must be tackled on a daily basis.

Because there is agritourism around the world, many opportunities are available. Tourists can spend the weekend at a farm in the California mountains where they learn how to milk a cow and make cheese, but they can also take tea plantation tours in Taiwan, gather figs at a fig farm in Spain, and enjoy many other experiences where they can be close to nature.

Overall, ranches and farms welcome agritourism. One American study found that in the state of Virginia alone, agritourism supported more than 20,000 jobs and generated $840 million in income. It has been a big step forward in keeping the farming industry alive.

B **IDENTIFY SPECIFIC INFORMATION** **Read the article again. Then answer the questions.**

1 How do tourists benefit from agritourism? ______

2 How does the farm industry benefit from agritourism? ______

3 Why has the farming economy suffered in recent years? ______

4 What states and countries are mentioned where tourists can experience agritourism? ______

5 How did agritourism benefit the state of Virginia? ______

C **IDENTIFY SPECIFIC INFORMATION** **Read the article again. Find three agritourism activities a tourist may experience.**

______

2 CRITICAL THINKING

A **THINK CRITICALLY** **Why do you think the agritourism industry has become so successful? Would you be interested in an agritourism experience? Why or why not?**

______

3 WRITING

A **The extracts are from an opinion essay about tourism. They are the beginning of each of the four paragraphs. Decide which paragraph each extract belongs in: first, second, third, or fourth.**

1 Another problem is the impact of tourists on the environment. For example, one beach in Thailand is so popular that tourists create more garbage than the island can cope with. As a result, a lot of plastic, cans, and other damaging items end up in the ocean.

Paragraph: ____________

2 Tourists around the world tend to visit the same places again and again. Everyone wants to see Times Square in New York City or the Grand Palace in Bangkok. However, I think visiting these popular destinations should be discouraged. Too many tourists in one place causes a lot of problems.

Paragraph: ____________

3 Of course, it's understandable that tourists want to see popular places because they are interesting. However, it's time to think more about the problems that welcoming too many tourists can cause.

Paragraph: ____________

4 The first reason tourists should consider non-popular destinations is because of overcrowding.

Paragraph: ____________

B **Complete the chart below with the advantages and disadvantages of tourism in a popular destination. Then write a paragraph about whether you agree or disagree that too much tourism can have a negative effect. Use *the first* and *the second,* or *first, next,* and *then* to organize your ideas.**

Advantages	Disadvantages

CHECK AND REVIEW

Read the statements. Can you do these things?

UNIT 1	Mark the boxes. ☑ I can do it. ? I am not sure. **I can …**	If you are not sure, go back to these pages in the Student's Book.
VOCABULARY	☐ **describe dealing with change.** ☐ **describing annoying things.**	page 2 page 4
GRAMMAR	☐ **use the simple present and the present continuous to describe past habits.** ☐ **express annoyance.**	page 3 page 5
LISTENING AND SPEAKING SKILLS	☐ **listen for opinions.** ☐ **use expressions for discussing views on issues.**	page 6 page 7
READING AND WRITING SKILLS	☐ **identify main ideas and specific information.** ☐ **organize information in an opinion essay.**	page 8 page 9

UNIT 2 NATURAL LIMITS

2.1 DEEP OCEAN OR DEEP SPACE?

1 VOCABULARY: Space and ocean exploration

A **Circle the correct word to complete the sentences.**

1 Some companies think they will be able to *launch* / *monitor* tourists into space within the next few years.
2 The researchers want to *use up* / *preserve* the natural beauty of the ocean.
3 Some experts are worried that humans will *use up* / *come across* the Earth's supply of oil one day.
4 I bought a telescope so I can *preserve* / *observe* the stars at night.
5 The equipment used to *monitor* / *come across* the ocean floor is very expensive.
6 Underwater vehicles are often used for ocean *exploration* / *atmosphere*.
7 Sometimes, *resources* / *satellites* are used to predict the weather.
8 Scientists are continuing their *resources* / *investigation* into why the rocket exploded upon take-off.
9 Too much pollution can create a dirty and unpleasant *atmosphere* / *species*.
10 The ocean contains many useful *resources* / *investigations*, such as salt, sand, copper, and oil.
11 Many *species* / *satellites* that live in the ocean are still being studied by scientists.
12 The tourists didn't *launched* / *come across* any rare type of fish on their boat trip.
13 I love to float on the *atmosphere* / *surface* of the water. It's so relaxing.

2 GRAMMAR: Comparative structures

A **Circle the correct word to complete each sentence.**

1 I prefer learning about recently discovered plants in the ocean rather than ______ for new types of fish.
   a to search   (b) searching
2 The idea of creatures living on Mars isn't realistic enough ______ searching for them.
   a to continue   b continuing
3 It is less important to find new species ______ it is to save the ones we already know about.
   a then   b than
4 In the future, there will be more jobs in ocean research than ______ space exploration.
   a in   b will be
5 I usually learn more about animals from going to museums ______ I do from watching movies.
   a than   b then
6 There is more water on the surface of the earth ______ land.
   a than   b than is

B **Correct the mistake in each sentence.**

1 She teaches ~~less~~ *fewer* lessons on space than she does on the ocean.
2 It seems like there is less money available for space exploration then for ocean exploration.
3 Traveling to Mars isn't safe enough justifying sending humans there yet.
4 It's much simpler to explore the ocean then to explore space.
5 The final exam on the stars and the planets was difficult than the English exam.
6 I prefer watching movies about space exploration rather than read about it.

3 GRAMMAR AND VOCABULARY

A **Answer the questions with complete sentences. Explain your answers.**

1 Which is more important: observing the effects of space on humans or finding life on other planets?

______

2 Should scientists focus more on preserving the ocean's environment than on discovering new species?

______

3 Is the International Space Station useful enough to spend government resources on?

______

4 Should more researchers be exploring the earth's oceans?

______

2.2 EXTREME LIFE

1 VOCABULARY: The natural world

A **Cross out the word that is different in meaning.**

1	territory	area	~~border~~
2	sea life	sand	fish
3	plant life	creature	tree
4	origin	creation	destination
5	habitat	environment	pond
6	adaptable	fixed	flexible
7	pond	habitat	lake
8	animal life	volcano	frog

B **(Circle) the correct word to complete each sentence.**

1 Camels can live for months in the desert without drinking water. They are ______ .
  a plant life b endangered (c) survivors
2 The villagers did not hear the noise from the ______ , but they saw smoke rising in the sky.
  a animal life b volcano c environment
3 Scientists are trying to identify the new ______ they discovered in the river.
  a territory b origin c form of life
4 Cutting down trees in a forest can harm an animal's natural ______ .
  a environment b creature c pond
5 Some berries in the forest are ______ . They can make you very sick.
  a poisonous b plant life c adaptable
6 The Asian elephant is one of the most famous ______ animals. There are fewer than 50,000 of them left on the planet.
  a poisonous b endangered c adaptable
7 Mosquitos are my least favorite ______ . They usually head straight for me even if other people are around.
  a habitats b origins c creatures

2 GRAMMAR: Superlative structures; ungradable adjectives

A **Complete each sentence with a phrase in the box.**

absolutely freezing	completely terrifying	least amount
~~least poisonous~~	most dangerous animals	smallest bird

1 The *least poisonous* snake is called the rat snake. Its bite may hurt, but it isn't deadly.

2 The ______ that scientists have found is called the bee hummingbird.

3 Greenland is one of the coldest places on Earth. It is ______, especially in the winter.

4 Crocodiles are one of the ______ in the world. They kill hundreds of people each year.

5 An active volcano is a/an ______ thing to see.

6 The ______ of sleep a typical adult needs to stay healthy is around six to seven hours per night.

B **Complete the sentences with phrases from the box and your own ideas.**

absolutely awful	most / least adaptable	most / least colorful	most / least dangerous	most / least enjoyable
most / least interesting	most / least pleasant	most / least unique	most / least unlikely	

1 The ______ fish in the ocean is the ______.

2 Places with a lot of sun are the ______ places to live.

3 ______ are one of the ______ insects on Earth.

4 ______ are one of the ______ animals to see in their natural habitat.

5 The ______ animal in the world is the ______.

6 The ______ threat to endangered animals is ______.

3 GRAMMAR AND VOCABULARY

A **Complete the sentences about three of the life forms in the box. Use vocabulary from exercises 1A and 1B, superlative structures, and ungradable adjectives.**

cockroaches	great white shark	kangaroos
king cobra	~~octopus~~	

1 *The octopus is the strangest and most beautiful form of sea life.*

2 ______

3 ______

4 ______

2.3 FINDING OUT

1 LISTENING

A 2.01 **What activities are the people in the photos doing? What is the same about the two activities? What is different? Listen to the conversation and check your answers.**

B 2.01 LISTEN FOR DETAILS **Listen to the conversation again. Complete the sentences with the correct number.**

1 As a beginner, Felix will most likely dive in about ____________ meter(s) of water.

2 A scuba diving oxygen tank lasts for ____________ hour(s).

3 There are ____________ steps to getting certified for scuba diving.

4 Felix will have to complete ____________ dive(s) as part of his certification process.

2 CRITICAL THINKING

A THINK CRITICALLY **How do you think scuba diving could be beneficial to the environment? How could it be dangerous to the environment?**

____

____

____

3 SPEAKING

A **Underline the expressions that ask for or provide specific information in each of the sentences below. Then match the questions to the answers.**

1 What exactly do you mean by saying tigers are endangered? ____
2 Is there any danger of the earth being overpopulated someday? ____
3 Would you recommend living in a desert climate? ____
4 Will tourists travel to space someday? ____
5 Is there a risk of injury when scuba diving? ____

a Maybe. One thing to keep in mind is the lack of rain.
b No. First and foremost, it will be too expensive.
c A small one, but it's generally a safe activity.
d There is a risk they will no longer exist someday.
e Yes, some experts say it will happen by the year 2050.

B **Read the situation below. Write three questions and then give three pieces of information. Remember to use phrases for exchanging information.**

Think of a city you've never been to but would like to go to. Imagine you are planning a trip to that city. You have a friend who recently went there, and you want to ask your friend for information. Write three questions you want to ask.

1 ____
2 ____
3 ____

Now, imagine your friend wants to visit a city you know. What three pieces of information would you give to your friend?

1 ____
2 ____
3 ____

2.4 EXTREME LIVING

1 READING

A **Look at the picture. Why do people like to watch survival reality shows? Read the article from an entertainment blog. Does it mention your ideas?**

Home Shows About

ONLY THE STRONG SURVIVE—And Get Paid For It

Why do we watch television shows where people are obviously uncomfortable? For about the last ten years, shows based on surviving in extreme environments have become very popular. In fact, there are currently more than 50 survival reality shows on television around the world.

These shows usually follow a basic structure. A group of strangers is dropped off in a remote location with limited, or no, supplies. They have to find food, water, and a safe place to sleep each night. Every week, the people on the show vote to remove one member of the group. The last remaining survivor usually wins money and prizes, sometimes up to $1 million.

Sometimes, there are only two people rather than a large group. They are allowed to select one tool, such as a sharp knife or something to help start a fire. They then have three weeks to walk to a new location, where food, water, and a ride home will be waiting for them. This becomes a lesson in working as a team and being patient under extreme circumstances.

Locations for survival reality shows are usually extreme; for example, the jungles of Micronesia, where the average annual rainfall is 100 to 200 inches (2540–5080 mm). The temperatures often reach over 100°F (38° C). One thing to keep in mind in these tropical climates is insects. People usually wake up with enormous mosquito bites, which add to other physical problems such as hunger and thirst.

Perhaps we watch these programs because we want to see how far people can push themselves, or we want to watch others have adventures that we'll never experience. Maybe we want to see them succeed, or maybe we're hoping they'll fail. Whatever the reason, it looks like people will be watching survival reality shows for a long time!

B **UNDERSTAND NUMERICAL WORDS AND PHRASES** **Read the article again. Read the statements. Then write *T* (true) or *F* (false).**

1 There are approximately 50 survival reality shows on television. ______
2 Contestants often win more than $1 million. ______
3 It usually rains up to 100 inches per year in Micronesia. ______
4 Temperatures might be higher than 100°F some days. ______

2 CRITICAL THINKING

A **THINK CRITICALLY** **Read the article again. What kind of information do the numbers in the text give?**

______

______

______

3 WRITING

A **USE NUMERICAL WORDS AND PHRASES** **Think of a city or town that you would like to visit. Answer the questions about the place you chose. You will need to look up some information online.**

1 What is the population?

2 What is the average yearly rainfall?

3 What is the average yearly snowfall?

4 Describe the range of temperatures.

5 Describe the environment.

B **Write a paragraph that describes the place you chose in exercise 3A. Use numerical words and phrases, and noun + *-like*. Explain why you would like to visit and what makes it interesting.**

CHECK AND REVIEW

Read the statements. Can you do these things?

UNIT 2	Mark the boxes. ☑ I can do it. ? I am not sure. **I can …**	If you are not sure, go back to these pages in the Student's Book.
VOCABULARY	☐ **describe space and ocean exploration.** ☐ **talk about life forms in the natural world.**	page 12 page 14
GRAMMAR	☐ **use comparative structures.** ☐ **use superlative structures and ungradable adjectives.**	page 13 page 15
LISTENING AND SPEAKING SKILLS	☐ **listen for details.** ☐ **use expressions to exchange information.**	page 16 page 17
READING AND WRITING SKILLS	☐ **understand numerical words and phrases.** ☐ **write a description of an area.**	page 18 page 19

UNIT 3 THE WAY I AM

3.1 POWER IN QUIET

1 VOCABULARY: Describing personality

A **Complete each conversation with a phrase in the box.**

attract attention	enjoy the company of	speak softly
speak up	the life of the party	

1 A Anna tells great stories about her world travels. People are always fascinated by them.
B Yeah, she sure is ______________ .

2 A Why are you sitting in the back of the classroom?
B I didn't do my homework, so I don't want to ______________ to myself.

3 A Can I come to the library with you to study?
B Sure, but we'll have to ______________ so we don't disturb people.

4 A Do you spend time with your co-workers outside of work?
B Sure. I really ______________ my coworkers. They've become my friends.

5 A You have creative ideas. You should ______________ more in meetings.
B Thanks! That's good advice. I'll try to say more from now on.

B **Circle the correct word to complete each sentence.**

1 Robert wasn't invited to the movies, so he *felt left out* / *was an introvert*.
2 Each time you *show off* / *interact with* a native speaker, your English will improve.
3 Even if you're *an extrovert* / *an introvert*, it's important to spend time with friends to avoid being alone too often.
4 Whenever we go to a party, Jorge loves to *show off* / *interact with* his dance moves.
5 If I leave my cell phone at home, I'm more likely to *socialize* / *be reserved*. That way, I meet a lot of new people.
6 At school, Jun chats with his friends a lot. It's obvious he *feels left out* / *is an extrovert*.

2 GRAMMAR: Relative pronouns; reduced relative clauses

A **Combine the sentences to make one sentence.**

1 Wednesday is one day of the week. I have time to go to my exercise class.
Wednesday is one day of the week when I have time to go to my exercise class.

2 You can read the book. I bought the book yesterday.
____

3 She brought her dog on vacation with her. Her dog's name is Duke.
____

4 Valentina invited 50 people to her party. Valentina loves celebrating her birthday with her friends.
____

5 I ate lunch at a restaurant. The restaurant was voted the best restaurant in the city.
____

B Circle the correct word to complete each sentence.

1 My favorite time of year is summer vacation, ______ to a lot of parties.
   a when invited   b which I get invited   (c) when I get invited
2 Some introverts prefer to live in small cities, ______ than large cities.
   a that are less crowded   b which are less crowded   c less crowded
3 My best friend grew up in a small town ______ Friendship.
   a where is called   b which calling   c called
4 People ______ social media often say they enjoy making new friends online.
   a who use   b use   c when they use
5 The speaker, ______ is about the effects of social media, gave an interesting presentation.
   a whose research   b which research   c who research
6 There are many studies ______ being alone too often is bad for a person's health.
   a say   b that say   c that saying

3 GRAMMAR AND VOCABULARY

A Complete each sentence with a word in the box. You may use a word more than once. Then write a sentence that is true for you using the same relative clause structure.

called	that	where	~~which~~	who	whose

1 a I like to show off my musical skills, *which* often makes me the life of the party.
  b I like to *show off my cooking skills, which makes me popular with my friends*.
2 a I'm a person ______ enjoys the company of strangers.
  b I'm a person ______.
3 a Being an introvert is a trait ______ should get more respect.
  b Being an introvert ______.
4 a In class, ______ I'm more reserved, I don't speak up very often.
  b In class, ______.
5 a Socializing regularly is an activity ______ I value.
  b Socializing ______.
6 a I'm someone ______ friends are mostly extroverts.
  b I'm someone ______.
7 a All of my classmates liked the information session ______ "How to succeed in college."
  b All of my classmates ______.

B Write a description of a person you know well. Use relative clauses and words to describe his or her personality.

3.2 THINGS AND EMOTIONS

1 VOCABULARY: Strong feelings

A **Put the words in the correct places in the chart. You will use one word twice.**

~~bizarre~~	creepy	disgusting	~~fabulous~~	impressive	irritating
satisfying	stunning	tense	uneasy	weird	

Positive	Negative
fabulous	bizarre

B **Circle the correct words to complete the sentences.**

1 Overall, my semester was *stunning* / *satisfying*. I liked my professors and I learned a lot.
2 Animals tend to feel *disgusting* / *uneasy* before natural disasters, such as earthquakes.
3 Almost everyone agrees that her book is *fabulous* / *irritating*. It has won many awards.
4 The floor of the restaurant is *weird* / *disgusting*. There is food and dirt everywhere.
5 Therese feels *tense* / *fabulous* driving at night because she can't see very well.
6 Do you think my dress is *weird* / *uneasy*? I made it myself.
7 Those people in the theater were *impressive* / *irritating*. They talked throughout the entire movie.
8 I used to think broccoli was *creepy* / *gross*, but now it's one of my favorite vegetables.
9 The man's behavior was *bizarre* / *satisfying*, so no one wanted to sit next to him.
10 There is a *stunning* / *creepy* view of the city on top of that building.
11 Anthony gave a/an *weird* / *impressive* speech, which encouraged people to donate money.
12 I love stories about ghosts, even though I find them *satisfying* / *creepy*.

2 GRAMMAR: Present participles

A **Match the sentence halves.**

1 As a manager working at a large corporation, ___c___
2 Some people like to take the bus, ______
3 Today, I'm spending time with my childhood friends, ______
4 Abraham loves to sit on his porch alone, ______
5 The people ______
6 This weekend I'm relaxing, ______
7 The sight of someone ______

a talking about the old days.
b eating makes me hungry.
c Lara works a lot of hours.
d catching up on things I don't have time to do during the week.
e using the time to read or study.
f drinking coffee and enjoying the peace.
g earning the most money donate generously.

B **Complete the sentences with the correct form of the verbs in parentheses.**

1 I get annoyed by ___sitting___ (sit) in traffic, ___waiting___ (wait) for the cars to move.
2 The plane ______ (arrive) from Paris was early, which ______ (make) everyone happy.
3 We ______ (try) the new restaurant, ______ (expect) an excellent meal.
4 As someone ______ (work) in the movie industry, I ______ (watch) a lot of films.
5 The sight of the car ______ (drive) quickly toward me was frightening.
6 She loved ______ (attend) the concert, ______ (listen) to her favorite singer.

3 GRAMMAR AND VOCABULARY

A **Complete the sentences so that they are true for you.**

1 As a child living in ______, I thought ______ was fabulous.
2 As a student studying English, I think ______ is satisfying.
3 It's impressive to dance while ______.
4 Animals eating ______ is disgusting.
5 The sound of people ______ is irritating.

B **Complete the sentences. Use present participles.**

1 ______ makes me uneasy.
2 ______ is stunning.
3 ______ looks bizarre.
4 ______ smells weird.
5 ______ sounds creepy.
6 ______ makes me tense.

3.3 ASKING FOR FAVORS

1 LISTENING

A 3.01 LISTEN FOR INFERENCE **Listen to the conversations. Then answer the questions.**

Conversation 1

1 What does Sam say to show that he's uneasy about taking the personality test?

2 What is the likely relationship between Yulia and Sam?

Conversation 2

3 Do you think Gabrielle has experience in the business world? Why or why not?

4 Do you think Gabrielle is an introvert or an extrovert? Explain your answer.

B 3.01 **Listen to the conversation again. Then answer the questions.**

Conversation 1

1 Why does Sam think he might not be able to help Yulia?

2 What does Yulia say that makes Sam feel better about taking the test?

Conversation 2

3 What does Fernanda say to show she supports Gabrielle's idea to be a health coach?

4 Does Fernanda agree to give Gabrielle money for her business? What does she say?

2 CRITICAL THINKING

A THINK CRITICALLY **What do you think a personality test might reveal about a person? What do you think a personality test might say about you? Would you feel comfortable sharing the results with strangers?**

3 SPEAKING

A **Answer the requests with phrases from the box and your own ideas. More than one answer may be correct. Use each phrase at least once.**

I don't know how much I'd be able to …	I don't mean to be rude, but …
I'd be happy to help you out.	Sorry but I wouldn't be comfortable …
~~Yes, I can probably manage that.~~	

1 **A** Is there any chance you could give me a ride to work tomorrow?
B Yes, I can probably manage that. I'll pick you up at 8 a.m.

2 **A** Do you think it would be possible for me to see your notes from class?
B ______________________ didn't you take your own notes in class today?

3 **A** Would you be willing to lend me some money?
B ______________________ How much do you need?

4 **A** Is there any chance you could teach me the new software program?
B ______________________ I don't really know how the new software works.

5 **A** Do you think it would be possible for me to borrow your car?
B ______________________ lending you my car. I'm usually the only one who drives it.

6 **A** I found a new apartment. Would you be willing to help me move?
B ______________________ When is your moving date?

B **Complete the conversations with phrases from the box in exercise 3A.**

1 **Boss** Is there any chance you could work late tonight?
Employee ______________________

2 **Roommate A** Do you think it would be possible for my friend Jack to move in with us?
Roommate B ______________________

3 **Classmate A** Would you be willing to explain the teacher's lecture to me? I didn't understand most of it.
Classmate B ______________________

3.4 THE RIGHT JOB FOR ME

1 READING

A **Read the job names in the article. Name one thing a person who works each of the jobs might typically do. Then read the article and check your answers.**

Get Out of Your Comfort Zone at Work

For some people, a typical work day includes sitting at a desk, taking phone calls, and tapping away at a computer. However, there are plenty of more unusual careers for people who want something a little different. Would you like to interact with poisonous snakes, study emoji icons, or eat ice cream all day and get paid for it? Read about three unique jobs and see if they are right for you.

EMOJI TRANSLATOR

Emojis have become so effective in communicating emotions that international corporations now use them to connect with clients. But just as human body language varies across cultures, so do expressions and gestures communicated by emojis. For example, the thumbs-up sign may be positive in the United States, but it is insulting in Russia. Companies are now hiring emoji translators who report on how emojis can cause problems in different cultures.

ICE CREAM TASTER

John Harrison starts his work day at 7:30 a.m. when his taste buds are at their sharpest. He then samples around 20 ice cream flavors, which he analyzes for taste and smell. It's not as easy as it sounds, though. Harrison's formal job title is "flavorologist." People who would like to have this dream-like career should have experience in food science, product development, and maybe even chemistry. They must have an excellent sense of taste, and they may also be responsible for inventing new ice cream flavors.

SNAKE MILKER

Are you uneasy around snakes? Then this job definitely isn't for you. A snake milker extracts poisonous venom from snakes, which is then used to develop treatments for medical conditions. Someone holding this job must be comfortable caring for snakes, making sure they are not harmed in the process. Snake milkers usually have degrees in animal biology, and they may work in research labs, universities, and zoos.

B IDENTIFY AUDIENCE **Read the article again. Then answer the questions.**

1 Who is the audience for the text?
 a high school students
 b people who like their jobs
 c people looking for a career change

C **How do you think most readers would feel about each job?**

1 emoji translator ______________________
2 ice cream taster ______________________
3 snake milker ______________________

2 CRITICAL THINKING

A THINK CRITICALLY **Would you like to work at any of the jobs mentioned in the article? Why or why not? Is there another unusual job you'd like to have?**

____

____

____

3 WRITING

A **Think of *five* words or phrases that describe your personality and give a specific example that illustrates each word or phrase.**

B **Look online for a job you would be interested in applying for. Think about skills you have that are relevant for the job.**

C **Write a personal statement for the job you chose in exercise 3B. It should highlight your skills and personality, explaining why they would make you suitable for the job. Use *in order to* in your answer.**

CHECK AND REVIEW

Read the statements. Can you do these things?

UNIT 3	Mark the boxes. ✔ I can do it. ? I am not sure. **I can …**	If you are not sure, go back to these pages in the Student's Book.
VOCABULARY	☐ **describe personality types.** ☐ **express things I like and don't like.**	page 22 page 24
GRAMMAR	☐ **use relative clauses to add description to sentences.** ☐ **use present participles to describe two events happening at the same time.**	page 23 page 25
LISTENING AND SPEAKING SKILLS	☐ **listen for inference.** ☐ **role play making and responding to requests.**	page 26 page 27
READING AND WRITING SKILLS	☐ **identify audience for a text.** ☐ **write a personal statement.**	page 28 page 29

UNIT 4 COMBINED EFFORT

4.1 IT TAKES A TEAM

1 VOCABULARY: Professional relationships

A **Circle the correct definition of the word in bold.**

1 As a restaurant owner, I **oversee** every aspect of the business.
  (a) watch to make certain something is done correctly
  b ask someone for help or advice
2 Role models, such as famous writers or athletes, often **contribute** to a person's success in life.
  a accept responsibility for
  b give something
3 I couldn't decide which jobs I wanted to apply for, so I **turned to** a career counselor for help.
  a asked someone for help or advice
  b helped someone
4 Frances received a large grant to **assist** her in her research.
  a show or prove that something is true
  b help
5 In order to get the job, Ruth had to **demonstrate** that she could work well on a team.
  a watch to make certain something is done correctly
  b show or prove that something is true

B **Complete the paragraph with the words in the box.**

acts as	build a relationship	build trust
enables us to	~~keep an eye on~~	steer everyone away from

I come from a family with three kids. My sister Annie is the youngest. She's only seven, so we all have to [1] *keep an eye on* her. Monica is the oldest, which means she often [2] ________ our boss, even when our parents are around! I'm in the middle, so it's my job to [3] ________ arguing with each other. Our parents often tell us how important siblings are because we [4] ________ with each one of them, and those relationships will be our models throughout our lives. They also tell us it's important to [5] ________ with each other. That [6] ________ always have people in our lives to rely on.

2 GRAMMAR: Adding emphasis: *so … that*, *such … that*, *even*, *only*

A **Complete the sentences with *even* or *only*.**

1 I ________ need a little more money to buy the car of my dreams.
2 She can speak four languages, ________ Mandarin, which I find really difficult.
3 I'm so busy I don't ________ have time to cook.
4 I ________ trust one person and that's my best friend.
5 The company is growing so fast that their ________ focus is to hire more people.

B **Choose the correct words or phrases to complete each sentence.**

1 It was ______ movie that I left before it was over.

a so scary (b) such a scary

2 She was ______ that she fell asleep on the subway.

a so much tired b so tired

3 Rita ______ has a month to go before she finishes law school.

a only b even

4 Hyun has ______ homework that he has to stay up all night to finish it.

a so much b such

5 I'm ______ that I don't think I'll ever eat again!

a so full b such full

6 The snow was so heavy that I couldn't ______ see where the road was.

a only b even

7 Francis is ______ intelligent that he was accepted to all the best colleges.

a so b such

3 GRAMMAR AND VOCABULARY

A **Use the information to write new sentences. Use the words in parentheses to add emphasis.**

1 Adam's teacher keeps an eye on him at all times. (so … that)

Adam is so lazy in class that his teacher keeps an eye on him at all times.

2 Vera was a good temporary department manager. (such … that)

3 My friends steer me away from bad decisions. (only)

4 That woman contributes money to the school every year. (so … that)

5 Mariah has very little money. She cannot pay the rent. (even)

6 I've built a strong relationship with my sister. (such … that)

7 It was difficult to demonstrate the new computer system. (so … that)

8 I oversee one small department of employees. (only)

4.2 DESTRUCTIVE TEAMS

1 VOCABULARY: Assessing ideas

A **Cross out the word that is different in meaning.**

1 valid	~~illegal~~	acceptable
2 destructive	productive	harmful
3 weakness	imperfection	advantage
4 aspect	part	whole
5 point out	hide	tell
6 assess	study	ignore
7 constructive	negative	useful

B **Complete the sentences with the words and phrases in the box.**

consequence	draw attention to
strength	~~think through~~
unreasonable	weigh the pros and cons

1 Lucas needs to ___think through___ his job offer. The job would require him to move across the country, so it's a big decision.

2 When making a major decision, it's necessary to ________________. There are good and bad points to everything.

3 Being decisive is usually considered a/an ________________ in the business world.

4 It is ________________ to ask people to work more than five days per week.

5 In my presentation, I plan to ________________ the problem of unemployment in our city. I want to make sure the audience is aware of it.

6 As a/an ________________ of missing the final exam, Haewon failed the class.

2 GRAMMAR: Reflexive pronouns; pronouns with *other/another*

A **Circle the correct form of *other/another*.**

1 I got to the restaurant before everyone else. *The others / The other* hadn't arrived yet.
2 Every successful relationship requires respecting *one another / the other.*
3 Our team is too small to get the job done. We need *other / another* person.
4 I have two sisters. One is a lawyer and *the other / another* is a judge.
5 When the *other / others* arrive, we'll begin the meeting.

B **Complete the sentences with a reflexive pronoun.**

1 Before you say yes, ask ___yourself___ if you really want to take on another project.
2 He enjoys going to the movies by ______.
3 Our team won the championship. We should be proud of ______.
4 The computer will shut ______ down in one hour.
5 She finally bought ______ a new car.
6 Are you and Dana going to leave ______ enough time to finish the project?
7 Before looking for a new job, he asked ______ what his strengths and weaknesses were.

3 GRAMMAR AND VOCABULARY

A **Answer the questions with information so that is true for you. Use complete sentences. Use reflexive pronouns, pronouns with *other/another*, and vocabulary from exercises 1A and 1B.**

1 When are the opinions of others more valid than your own opinions?

______

______

2 How can spending too much time by yourself have negative consequences?

______

______

3 Has another person ever told you that you were being unreasonable?

______

______

4 When was the last time you had to really think something through?

______

______

4.3 TWO PEOPLE, ONE JOB

1 LISTENING

A 4.01 LISTEN FOR ATTITUDE **Listen and answer the questions.**

1 What attitude does Katrina have?

a helpful b happy c negative

2 What attitude do the audience members have?

a angry b positive c concerned

3 How certain is Katrina that her company retreat will be successful?

a very certain b partly certain c not very certain

4 How does Katrina respond to the audience's questions?

a with doubt b with reassurance c with impatience

B 4.01 **Listen again. Circle the correct answer.**

1 Katrina's company offers:

a one-day retreats b seven-day retreats c a variety of retreats

2 Katrina points out that employees on retreats might worry about:

a being bored b their schedule c their clients

3 According to Katrina, the benefits of retreats include:

a playing games b building trust c missing work

4 Katrina helps with:

a scheduling b looking after other clients c having fun

2 CRITICAL THINKING

A THINK CRITICALLY **Make a list of the advantages and disadvantages of a company retreat. What are some games or activities that would help build relationships at a company retreat?**

3 SPEAKING

A **Put the conversation in order.**

_____ **A** Oh, no. I'd be concerned that I would get lost if I traveled by myself.

_____ **B** That's right, Angela. I'm leaving in a few weeks. I'll be gone for six months.

_____ **B** Well, the upside is that it makes you independent. If you get lost, you just figure it out on your own.

_____ **A** Aren't you worried about being lonely? Or bored?

_____ **A** That's true. I guess I have some unreasonable fears. I'm so worried about everything that I doubt I would have a good time. Well, have fun!

1 **A** Hi, Adrian. I heard you were planning to take a trip to South America by yourself.

_____ **B** No, not at all. The main benefit of traveling alone is that it's easy to build relationships with other travelers. Have you ever traveled alone?

B **Write a dialogue in which you try to convince your boss to let you do one of the following: take a year off to study a language abroad, work from home, or give you a raise. Use expressions for discussing advantages and disadvantages.**

You _____

_____

Your boss _____

You _____

_____

Your boss _____

You _____

_____

Your boss _____

4.4 THE ME TEAM

1 READING

A **Think of three benefits that playing team sports might have for children. Then read the article and check your ideas.**

Sports for Life

Team sports have the potential to play a vital role in a child's life. Of course, there are the health benefits that exercise brings. An active child is overall a happier, healthier child. Another plus is that sports expose children to the value of working on a team. They learn to solve problems better, and they build relationships with others. This aspect of team sports is important later in life, too, when they're ready to enter the workforce.

You might say that the downside of team sports is the possibility of losing. In fact, losing contributes to important life skills, too. Everyone loves to celebrate when their team wins. But imagine if your child's team has practiced and worked hard and is confident they're going to win the next game, but they end up losing. That would be a real disappointment, wouldn't it?

But that loss demonstrates to your child that a person can work hard at something and still not succeed. Children learn to keep trying and not to give up. They keep hoping for a more successful outcome. After all, losing isn't a weakness; it's an opportunity for improvement. It also teaches children to share their disappointment with their teammates, so they don't have to take on those negative feelings all by themselves.

Parents often worry about the downside of team sports. They argue that sports can take up a lot of time that their child could spend on academics. However, athletes actually do better in school. Because games like soccer, baseball, and football have specific and complicated rules, memorization and repeated practice are required. These are skills that carry over into learning a language, for example when you weigh the pros and cons, it's obvious that team sports are the clear winner.

B UNDERSTAND AUTHOR'S ATTITUDE **Read the article again. Then answer the questions.**

1 What is the author's attitude toward team sports?

a encouraging b pessimistic c undecided

2 Find three reasons to support your answer to Question 1.

1 ______
2 ______
3 ______

C **Read the article again. Answer the questions.**

1 What are three benefits of team sports that the author gives? ______

2 What does losing teach children? ______

3 How do team sports help a child's academic performance? ______

2 CRITICAL THINKING

A THINK CRITICALLY **Do you think that the benefits of children playing team sports outweigh the challenges? Why or why not?**

______

3 WRITING

A **Read the summary. Cross out the sentences that don't belong. Why don't the sentences belong in the summary?**

I recently read a book about a young man who grew up in the South of the United States. It was a true story. The author wrote about growing up in poverty and how it was a difficult life for him and his family. It also affected his performance in school. His grades suffered, and he almost dropped out of high school. I am glad his teachers helped him stay in school. He must have had good teachers who cared about him. The author finally graduated from high school and went on to college. While in college, he took a part-time job and was able to buy a car. When he graduated from college, he had excellent grades and he decided to go to law school. I don't know if I could ever finish law school because it sounds very difficult. After law school, he got a job and made enough money to help support his family. He felt very proud of the accomplishments he made in his life, even though it was a hard life at first.

B **SUMMARIZE MAIN POINTS Write a summary of the article on page 32. Decide if it's more appropriate to use *state* or *say* when you report the author's words.**

CHECK AND REVIEW

Read the statements. Can you do these things?

UNIT 4	Mark the boxes. ✔ I can do it. ? I am not sure. **I can …**	If you are not sure, go back to these pages in the Student's Book.
VOCABULARY	☐ **describe supportive people.** ☐ **use words and phrases to assess ideas.**	page 34 page 36
GRAMMAR	☐ **use expressions that add emphasis.** ☐ **use reflexive pronouns and forms of *other/another*.**	page 35 page 37
LISTENING AND SPEAKING SKILLS	☐ **listen for a speaker's attitude.** ☐ **discuss advantages and disadvantages.**	page 38 page 39
READING AND WRITING SKILLS	☐ **understand an author's attitude.** ☐ **summarize main points.**	page 40 page 41

UNIT 5 THE HUMAN FACTOR

5.1 IMITATING REALITY

1 VOCABULARY: Dealing with emotions

A **Complete the sentences with the words and phrases in the box.**

anxiety level	are rational	breathing technique	cure	~~overcome a fear~~	try a therapy

1 When you *overcome a fear*, you are no longer afraid of something.
2 When you ______ an illness, you make it better.
3 When your ______ is high, you feel nervous and upset.
4 When you ______, you can think about and explain things clearly.
5 When you are using a(n) ______, you might count your breaths.
6 When you ______, you should talk to an expert.

B **Circle the words or phrases to complete the sentences.**

1 When you *panic* / *calm down* you feel more relaxed.
2 You might *cure an illness* / *panic* when you take a test.
3 If you are *scared to death* / *conscious* of taking risks, you probably won't start a business.
4 If you *try a therapy* / *regain control*, you have power.
5 When you *overcome a fear* / *are conscious* of something, you are aware of it.
6 Usually, people *are in control* / *regain control* of their actions.

2 GRAMMAR: Real conditionals

A **Match the sentence halves.**

1 If you want to do yoga at home, *c*
2 When patients need medical advice at home, ____
3 My anxiety level becomes very high ____
4 I might take away my son's tablet ____
5 If you want to meet tomorrow, ____
6 I usually regain control of my emotions ____
7 Whenever I see a scary movie, ____
8 If I can't get over my fear of spiders, ____

a if he spends too much time online.
b I can't sleep at night.
c you could watch some videos.
d when I breathe deeply a few times.
e I may see a therapist.
f some doctors will talk to them on Skype.
g whenever I see a snake.
h you'll have to come to my office.

B **Check (✓) the correct sentences. Correct the incorrect sentences.**

1 If you're scared to death of something, listening to music might help you calm down. ✓

2 If I ~~will~~ decide to try a new therapy, I'll ask you to recommend a therapist. ☐

If I decide to try a new therapy, I'll ask you to recommend a therapist.

3 I use a breathing technique when my anxiety level was too high. ☐

4 When ever I panic about something, I imagine I am at the beach relaxing. ☐

5 If I can overcome my fear of crowded places, when I will go to the concert. ☐

6 When you will calm down maybe you'll be more rational. ☐

7 I might try to run a marathon if I can regain control of my health. ☐

8 Whenever I used my meditation app, I am more in control of my thoughts. ☐

9 When you're conscious of the source of your fear, it's easier to overcome it. ☐

10 Whenever I can cure my fear of heights, I may climb Mount Everest. ☐

3 GRAMMAR AND VOCABULARY

A **Read the situations below and give three suggestions for each one. Use real conditionals and the words in the boxes.**

1 Your friend dreams of going hiking in the jungles of Indonesia. However, your friend is terrified of snakes, and Indonesia is home to many poisonous snakes.

~~be scared to death~~	calm down	overcome a fear

a If you are scared to death, try to think of something positive instead.

b

c

2 Your friend tells you that every time he goes to a party, he feels anxious. He is nervous meeting new people.

be conscious of	be in control of	breathing technique

a

b

c

3 Your classmate is very intelligent, but she freezes every time she takes a test. She ends up getting a low grade.

anxiety level	panic	try a therapy

a

b

c

5.2 THE END OF THE OFFICE?

1 VOCABULARY: Willingness and unwillingness

A **Circle the correct words to complete the sentences.**

1 Alexandra ______ work at home because she doesn't think she would get a lot of work done.
   a is eager to **(b)** is reluctant to
2 Morgan ______ be his own boss. He likes making his own schedule and not having to explain his actions to anyone.
   a is more than happy to **b** has no desire to
3 I ______ communicate with coworkers via text message because I don't want to share my cell phone number.
   a am unwilling to **b** have no intention of
4 Alisha doesn't like to wake up early. She ______ change her work schedule.
   a hesitates to **b** is dying to
5 If an employee ______ driving to work every day, he or she might look for a job that involves working from home.
   a is passionate about **b** is against
6 When starting your own business at home, you have to ______ separate your work time from your leisure time, so that you don't work too much.
   a be prepared to **b** be anxious to

2 GRAMMAR: Conditionals: alternatives to *if*

A **Circle the correct words or phrases to complete the sentences.**

1 We can have our meeting via video call *(as long as)* / *unless* the internet connection is strong.
2 My boss said I can work at home *even if* / *providing* I come into the office once a month.
3 A company is successful *only if* / *even if* the employees are happy and productive.
4 I won't work from home *unless* / *providing that* I move to a bigger house.
5 I don't mind working in an office *even if* / *provided that* I can set my own schedule.
6 I love working at home and wouldn't go back to an office, *so long as* / *even if* you paid me more money.
7 I will invest in your business, but *only if* / *unless* you give me a percentage of your profits.
8 You can take a long vacation *unless* / *so long as* you finish your work before you go.

B **Complete the conversation in a job interview between the interviewer (A) and the candidate (B). Use the correct form of the phrases in parentheses.**

1 **A** ___Are___ you ___eager to___ work here? *(be eager to)*

2 **B** Yes. I ______ the work your company does. I want to work here even if I have to start at an entry level position. *(be passionate about)*

3 **A** ______ you ______ socialize outside of work, provided that it's an event that helps build relationships with your coworkers? *(be willing to)*

4 **B** Sure, I ______, so long as I don't have to stay out too late. *(be more than happy to)*

A Do you plan to continue your training in this field? For example, do you have any intention of getting a master's degree?

5 **B** Well, I ______ say yes to that because school is very expensive. I'd like to continue my training, but only if there was financial assistance. *(hesitate to)*

6 **A** If you work here, you will share an office with several of your coworkers. ______ you ______ that? *(be against)*

B That's fine with me. I don't mind sharing an office.

A Great! Are you ready to start work immediately?

7 **B** Yes, I ______ start tomorrow as long as you want to hire me. *(be prepared to)*

3 GRAMMAR AND VOCABULARY

A **Complete the sentences with your own ideas.**

1 I'm reluctant to go back to school even if ___my job pays for it___.

2 I'm eager to travel to foreign countries so long as ______.

3 I hesitate to find a new job unless ______.

4 I'm more than happy to help you with your problem, providing ______.

5 I have no desire to go to the gym unless ______.

6 I'm anxious to learn how to drive even if ______.

5.3 STOP BLAMING GAMING

1 LISTENING

A 5.01 LISTEN FOR SPEAKER'S DEGREE OF CERTAINTY **Listen to the podcast about banning technology in the home. Is the speaker certain or uncertain about his or her ideas? Listen to the language describing these ideas and check (✓)the ones that sound confident.**

☐ 1 **Ingrid** So yes, spending too much time online can lead to problems in a child's emotional development.

☐ 2 **Ingrid** Parents simply need to be conscious of how much time is spent online.

☐ 3 **Host** Their home is absolutely free of modern technology.

☐ 4 **Leon** You can bet those parents have inside knowledge about how companies make sure that kids want to use devices all the time.

☐ 5 **Leon** But who knows how long that calmness lasts?

B 5.01 **Listen to the podcast again. Then answer the questions.**

1 Why did Leon ban technology in his home?

2 What is 27% more likely to happen when teenagers use social media too often?

3 Why did Leon say the parents have "inside knowledge?" What is their "inside knowledge?"

4 What alternative does Ingrid suggest to a total technology ban?

5 How does Leon feel about a "no-tech" week?

2 CRITICAL THINKING

A THINK CRITICALLY **Whose view about banning technology in the home do you agree with the most? Why?**

3 SPEAKING

A **Complete the conversation with the expressions in the box. More than one answer may be correct.**

at the same time	I don't have a clue	I guarantee that	it's a well-known fact
on the contrary	that said	Who knows	you can bet that

Thomas I'm going on a complete digital detox. I'm not going to use anything internet-based for 30 days. 1 *I guarantee that* I'll be more focused afterwards.

Ivan Well, 2 ______ that too much screen time before bed negatively affects a person's sleep, so you'll also be more rested.

Thomas Exactly. And I'll have more free time. 3 ______? Maybe I'll learn a language or a musical instrument.

Ivan 4 ______, you might have *too* much free time. How do you plan to stay in touch with people?

Thomas 5 ______. I guess writing letters is a thing of the past. 6 ______, it might be a good way to connect with people more deeply.

Ivan 7 ______ it'll be tough at times. 8 ______, I don't think I could ever do it, and I respect you for trying.

B **Write a contrasting answer to each statement. Use the expressions from exercise 3A.**

1 When teenagers use social media too often, their risk of depression increases.
At the same time, it can be a good way to help shy kids interact with others.

2 People would be much happier if they didn't have to drive to their offices every day.
______

3 If people work at home, they may become lonely.
______

4 I guarantee that kids will complain if they can't use technology for one week.
______

5 I don't have a clue how you can work in the technology industry and not use technology.
______

5.4 WHAT LANGUAGE BARRIER?

1 READING

A **Read the article. Underline the formal and informal connecting expressions. As an article on a blog, should it be more formal?**

CULTURAL ETIQUETTE IN THE DIGITAL AGE

When we think of language barriers while traveling, one of the first images that we often think of is a lost traveler, gesturing wildly to a confused local person.

The lost traveler doesn't know the local language, nor does he or she understand that gestures can be culture-based, too. In the last decade or so, another barrier to being understood in a new culture has appeared—cell phone etiquette.

OK, imagine this situation. An American man is on the subway in Japan when his cell phone rings. He answers and has a brief conversation. He keeps his voice low, but he still senses that people are annoyed. Later, he learns that it's actually rude to talk on a cell phone in public places in Japan. There's not much he can do to correct his previous poor behavior, so the next time he rides the subway, he simply switches his phone to silent.

Cell phone use can cause problems in the same way a misunderstood word or gesture can. And in the same way, knowing the correct action depends on which culture you're dealing with.

Trying to catch up on phone calls during lunch? If you're eating, you'll be considered rude if the person on the other end is from the United Kingdom. Therefore, save your UK calls for after lunch.

With regards to answering calls in public places, it's acceptable in the United States; however, it's rude if you're in the middle of a face-to-face conversation. In China, on the other hand, you may be in for a surprise if your in-person conversation is interrupted when your friend takes a call from another person.

It's easy to create cultural barriers. That said, the best way to avoid them is to educate yourself whenever dealing with cultures different from your own.

GLOSSARY

etiquette (n) the set of rules or customs that control accepted behavior in particular social groups or social situations

gesture (n) the movement of the hands, arms, or head to express an idea or feeling

B UNDERSTAND PROBLEMS AND SOLUTIONS **Read the article again. How did the person on the subway in Japan correct his error?**

____

____

C **Read the article again. Circle the correct answer.**

1 When it comes to cell phones:
  - **a** etiquette is similar in most countries.
  - **b** something rude in one culture may be acceptable in another.
  - **c** it's alright to follow the culture you are from, no matter which country you're in.

2 The writer uses the example of the lost traveler to show that:
  - **a** everyone should speak a foreign language.
  - **b** everyone gets lost when they travel.
  - **c** not knowing language and etiquette can cause problems.

3 What effect does the phrase, "OK, imagine this" have?
  - **a** It asks the reader to picture a situation.
  - **b** It asks the reader to agree with a situation.
  - **c** It asks the reader to think of another example.

2 CRITICAL THINKING

A **What is your opinion of using cell phones in a public place? In what situations do you think this is acceptable or not acceptable?**

3 WRITING

A **Read the statements. Underline the organizing and connecting expressions. Then write *O* if it's an opinion and *F* if it's a fact.**

1 With regards to cell phones, children in the United States get their first one around age ten, on average. ___
2 That said, speaking loudly on a cell phone in public is rude. ___
3 So yes, cell phone etiquette varies from country to country. ___
4 As for the increased use of cell phones, Finland was the first country to have more cell phones than landlines. ___
5 OK, cell phones are a necessary part of life. ___

B STATE OPINION AND GIVE EXAMPLES **Write a paragraph about the use of cell phones in public. Give examples of times when it could be a problem, and how that problem could be solved. Use organizing and connecting expressions when possible.**

CHECK AND REVIEW

Read the statements. Can you do these things?

UNIT 5	Mark the boxes. ☑ I can do it. ? I am not sure. **I can …**	If you are not sure, go back to these pages in the Student's Book.
VOCABULARY	☐ **use phrases to discuss emotions.** ☐ **use phrases to explain willingness and unwillingness.**	page 44 page 46
GRAMMAR	☐ **use real conditionals for general facts and possible future situations.** ☐ **use conditionals with alternatives to *if*.**	page 45 page 47
LISTENING AND SPEAKING SKILLS	☐ **listen for phrases that express degrees of certainty.** ☐ **use expressions to discuss and contrast ideas.**	page 48 page 49
READING AND WRITING SKILLS	☐ **understand problems and solutions.** ☐ **state an opinion.**	page 50 page 51

UNIT 6 EXPECT THE UNEXPECTED

6.1 GOING VIRAL

1 VOCABULARY: Talking about fame

A **Match the sentences.**

1 There are a lot of negative comments about him on gossip websites. d
2 He works hard to tell people about problems in our society. ____
3 His name is on the front page of the newspaper today. ____
4 He will go to the party for a few minutes, but then he has to leave. ____
5 He can sing and dance, and he plays the piano. ____
6 Tens of thousands of people watch his video every week. ____

a He makes headlines.
b It gets hits.
c He raises awareness.
d He has a bad reputation.
e He makes concerts entertaining.
f He will make an appearance.

B **Circle the correct words to complete the sentences.**

1 They asked Colin to *make headlines* / *do the broadcast* since he was the only person with television experience.
2 You *have never heard of* / *raise awareness of* someone if you don't know the person's name.
3 You should do something kind if you want to *make an appearance* / *catch somebody's attention*.
4 In his speech, he plans to *get hits* / *praise his mother* for helping him succeed.
5 You might *have a good reputation* / *get publicity* if you do something terrible.
6 She never intended to *seek fame* / *praise somebody*; however, everyone in the world knows her name.

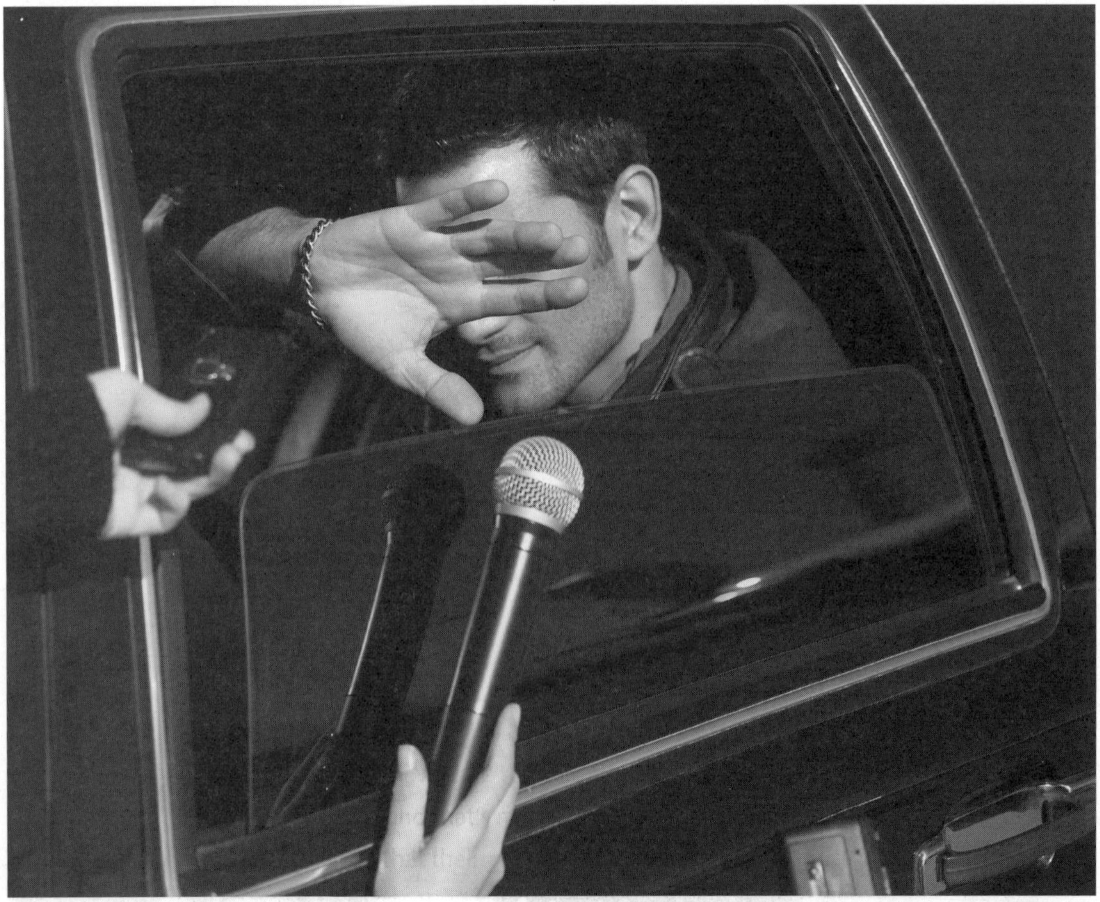

2 GRAMMAR: Narrative tenses

A **Circle the correct words to complete the sentence.**

1 He hadn't ______ for attention when he planned his cross-country bike ride.

(a) been looking **b** been looked **c** looks

2 As the man ______ the young girl, several people were recording it on their cell phones.

a rescuing **b** rescued **c** had rescued

3 She made her students laugh while she ______ her class.

a is teaching **b** taught **c** had taught

4 She had been an actor for ten years before people ______ recognizing her.

a had started **b** start **c** started

5 She had been taking care of animals for a long time before her story ______ in the news.

a appearing **b** appeared **c** had been appearing

6 People were already talking about her voice as she ______ the song.

a finishes **b** finishing **c** finished

B **Underline the event in each sentence that happens first. If the events happen at the same time, write *S* on the line.**

1 When Kiley was growing up, she didn't play any sports. ______

2 In high school, she was trying to get in shape, and she started playing on a basketball team. ______

3 She had been playing for about six months before someone wrote an article about her in a magazine. ______

4 Kylie helped her team win game after game, even though she had only been trying to get in shape. ______

5 Kylie hadn't planned on becoming famous before the article appeared in the magazine. ______

6 From then on, during her athletic career, she encouraged other young girls to play sports, too. ______

3 GRAMMAR AND VOCABULARY

A **Respond to *three* of the statements with information so that is true for you. Use the past continuous, past perfect, or past perfect continuous.**

1 Describe a situation where you or someone you know got a lot of hits on social media.

My friend had been putting pictures of her food on social media for about a year when she started to get a lot of hits.

2 Describe a time you or someone you know made headlines.

______

3 Describe how you caught your parents' attention when you were a child.

______

4 Describe a time when someone unexpected made an appearance at a big party or event.

______

5 Describe a situation in which you raised awareness of a social issue.

______

6.2 NOT AGAIN!

1 VOCABULARY: Reporting verbs

A **Circle the correct definitions.**

1 confirm
(a) to say that something is true
b to say that something is strange

2 hope to
a to want something to happen
b to say that something is true

3 announce
a to talk with too much pride about what you have done
b to tell a group of people about something

4 swear
a to say that you are sure something is true
b to pretend you don't know something

B **Cross out the word or phrase that is different in meaning.**

1	propose	suggest	~~remove~~
2	estimate	deceive	guess
3	have doubts about	be uncertain	be certain
4	insist	say firmly	forget
5	deny	accept	oppose

2 GRAMMAR: Reported speech with modal verbs

A **Check (✓) the correct sentences. Correct the incorrect sentences. Sentences should be in the past tense.**

1 I argued that we will need another month to complete the project. ☐
I argued that we would need another month to complete the project.

2 They explained that they might not come to the ceremony. ☐

3 They confirmed that they won't refund my money. ☐

4 We told everyone that they should come to our house early. ☐

5 He said he had doubts that he can show up on time. ☐

B **Rewrite the second line in each conversation as reported speech. Use a variety of reporting verbs.**

1 **Guest** Do you have any rooms available tonight?
Hotel employee No, sorry. We won't have a room free until tomorrow.
The hotel employee claimed they wouldn't have a room free until tomorrow.

2 **Customer** I forgot my wallet, so I'm afraid I can't pay the bill.
Waiter That's OK. You can come back tomorrow and pay.

3 **Mikhail** The subway isn't running. I don't know how I'm going to get to work.
Judi I might be able to help you.

3 GRAMMAR AND VOCABULARY

A **Rewrite the sentences in reported speech using the subject and verb in parentheses. Supply a subject for the sentences if necessary.**

1 "The new smartphones will go on sale next week." (the company / announce)

The company announced that the new smartphones would go on sale next week.

2 "We will arrive in Los Angeles on time." (pilot / claim)

3 "The meeting will start at 9:00 a.m." (my boss / confirm)

4 "I could do a better job if I were given the chance." (the young man / argue)

5 "The bus will not be late." (the driver / insist)

6 "I can make the best chocolate cake in the world." (the chef / boast)

B **Imagine you just moved into a new apartment. When you moved in, you found that the landlord had not done what he promised. Look at the conversation you had with the landlord and the problems below. Report the conversation to a friend. Use reporting verbs from the word box.**

claim	confirm	estimate	explain
insist	say	swear	tell

You Hmm, I don't think I like the bright green walls.

Landlord Oh, that's no problem. I can paint them white before you move in.

You OK. And are the neighbors upstairs noisy?

Landlord Oh, no. They're very quiet. You won't even know they're there!

You Great, but I don't see a refrigerator in the kitchen.

Landlord It's getting repaired and will be here soon. If it takes too long, I might just buy a new one.

You Sounds good. And what about the backyard? Can I use it whenever I want to?

Landlord Sure, it's all yours. You could even have parties and invite your friends.

Problems:

- He didn't paint the walls.
- The neighbors are very noisy.
- There's no refrigerator in the kitchen.
- The backyard is now full of old furniture.

First, the landlord claimed he could paint the walls before I moved in.

6.3 SOMETHING IN THE WATER

1 LISTENING

A **Listen to a conversation between Evelyn and Luisa. How do they know each other?**

a they're neighbors

b they're mother and daughter

c they're close friends

B 6.01 UNDERSTAND MEANING FROM CONTEXT **Listen to the conversation again. Guess the meaning of the words below. What clues helped you to work out their meaning?**

1 biscotti

guess: ____________________

clues: ____________________

2 dunking

guess: ____________________

clues: ____________________

3 love seat

guess: ____________________

clues: ____________________

4 brick and mortar

guess: ____________________

clues: ____________________

2 CRITICAL THINKING

A THINK CRITICALLY **What makes a good neighbor? Is Evelyn a good neighbor for coming to Luisa's house? Why or why not?**

____

____

____

3 SPEAKING

A **Put the conversation in order.**

____	**Ben**	You must have been hungry.
____	**Ben**	I assume they cancelled the party, and everyone went home.
____	**Jun**	The server brought our food on a tray, but because it was dark, he tripped and all of it went flying across the dining room. We waited another half an hour for new meals.
____	**Ben**	Uh-oh. What?
1	**Ben**	How was the anniversary party last night?
____	**Ben**	I suppose you fed everyone and saved the party.
____	**Jun**	Not at all. We lit candles, and someone used their smartphone to play music. But then something terrible happened.
____	**Jun**	To an extent, but you know I always have snacks hidden in my bag.
____	**Jun**	It was interesting. Because of the big storm, the power went out. It was totally dark inside the restaurant.

B **Write a short conversation for each situation below.**

1 You went to the airport to catch a flight for a business trip. You arrived on time for your flight, but when you went to check in, you realized you were at the wrong airport. You tell your coworker about it the next day.

You ______________________________

Your coworker ______________________________

You ______________________________

Your coworker ______________________________

You ______________________________

Your coworker ______________________________

You ______________________________

Your coworker ______________________________

2 You were working on a research paper when your computer crashed. You went to the school library to use one of the computers there, but it was closed. Your paper was due the next morning. You tell your classmate about it the next day.

You ______________________________

Your classmate ______________________________

You ______________________________

Your classmate ______________________________

You ______________________________

Your classmate ______________________________

You ______________________________

Your classmate ______________________________

6.4 GETTING IT WRONG

1 READING

A **Read the headline and the first paragraph of the story. What dream do you think came true for the writer? Read the story to check your answer.**

The dream that came true was: ______________________________

____

HOME ABOUT BLOG CONTACT US

A DREAM COME TRUE

It was my first time in New York City. I was with my best friend, and we wanted to see everything—Times Square, the Statue of Liberty …oh, and best of all, we had tickets to a Broadway musical. Neither of us had seen a live musical before, and we couldn't have been more excited. Years ago in high school, I was in the theater club, and I always dreamed of being a star.

On the evening of the performance, we had dinner near our hotel and then got on the subway. We had estimated that the subway ride to Broadway would take about 15 minutes. Thirty minutes later, we still weren't there.

When we finally arrived, we stood on the street looking around, and it certainly looked different from what I had imagined. First of all, I didn't see any tourists. Second, no theaters. I asked a woman for help. She told us that we were, indeed, at the Broadway subway station. Still confused, I showed her my ticket to the play. That's when it hit her.

We had taken the wrong subway to the wrong station and traveled to an entirely different area of New York City. There were no Broadway musicals anywhere near this Broadway station.

We thanked her and got into a taxi. I had heard that the theater didn't admit people if they were late, and I was panicking. When we hit traffic, the taxi driver insisted we'd get there faster if we got out and walked. He explained the best route and we jumped out and ran the rest of the way.

We arrived 20 minutes late, but they let us in. When we walked in, everyone in the audience turned to look at us.

I guess my dream of being the star of a Broadway show finally came true!

B **UNDERSTAND IRONY** **Read the story. Then answer the questions.**

1 How did the writer realize she had made a mistake?

____

2 What is ironic about the subway station they went to?

____

3 What is ironic about the writer's final sentence?

____

C **Read the story again. Then answer the questions.**

1 In high school, the writer:
  - a went to New York City.
  - b wanted to be a star.
  - c met her best friend.

2 When they got off the subway, the writer assumed:
  - a there would be more tourists.
  - b they were late for the play.
  - c they would be in Times Square.

3 The writer panicked because:
  - a the woman gave them the wrong information.
  - b the driver told them to get out of the taxi.
  - c they might not be let in to the theater.

2 CRITICAL THINKING

A **THINK CRITICALLY** **What do you think the writer and her friend did when the audience turned to look at them? What do you think the audience thought about them?**

____

____

3 WRITING

A **MAKE A STORY INTERESTING** **Read the story again. Underline examples of each of the points below.**

1 A variety of narrative verb tenses in the past.

2 Linking and organizing expressions.

3 Different kinds of sentences: conditionals *(if)*, relative clauses (*who, which*), time clauses (*when, after*), *There was/were*, reported speech, etc.

4 Reporting verbs other than *say*.

5 Two long sentences and two short sentences.

B **Write a story about one of the situations below. Use all of the writing points in exercise 3A to make your story interesting.**

1 Imagine that you and your friend got lost on a desert island for one week. Explain how you ate, where you slept, and how you found your way to safety. Describe some of the things you and your friend said during the week you were lost. ____

____

____

2 Tell a story about a time when you went to a large social event. Describe what people wore, ate, and talked about. ____

____

____

CHECK AND REVIEW

Read the statements. Can you do these things?

UNIT 6	Mark the boxes. ☑ I can do it. ? I am not sure. **I can …**	If you are not sure, go back to these pages in the Student's Book.
VOCABULARY	☐ **use expressions to talk about fame.** ☐ **use a variety of reporting verbs.**	page 54 page 56
GRAMMAR	☐ **use narrative tenses to tell a story.** ☐ **use reported speech with the correct form of modals.**	page 55 page 57
LISTENING AND SPEAKING SKILLS	☐ **guess the meaning of unfamiliar words from context.** ☐ **use expressions to make, contradict, and clarify. assumptions**	page 58 page 59
READING AND WRITING SKILLS	☐ **identify and understand irony.** ☐ **make a story interesting with a variety of grammar techniques.**	page 60 page 61

UNIT 7 PRIORITIES

7.1 WORTHY HELPERS

1 VOCABULARY: Positive experiences

A **Complete the sentences with the words in the box.**

beneficial	contribution	devote	~~difference~~	honor	influence
pleasure	reassure	satisfaction	use	value	worthwhile

1 I started a recycling program at school because I wanted to make a ___difference___.

2 The kid next door is a good ________ on Kevin.

3 Some people ________ their lives to serving their family, friends, and neighbors.

4 I needed my mother to ________ me that everything would be fine once I started college.

5 It was an ________ to have someone like him speak to the students.

6 Maybe his advice will be of ________ to you when you're older.

7 Many people take ________ in helping others.

8 She made an important ________ to today's meeting.

9 I ________ his friendship more than I could ever say.

10 She feels that teaching is a ________ career.

11 I get more ________ out of cooking than I do out of eating.

12 Drinking a lot of water is ________ for our health.

2 GRAMMAR: Gerunds and infinitives after adjectives, nouns, and pronouns

A **Match the sentence halves.**

1 It's unusual ___f___

2 Latin is an interesting language ____

3 Simon often wastes time ____

4 She has places ____

5 Valeria always feels nervous ____

6 We need someone ____

7 Samuel asked someone in class ____

8 It can be scary ____

a to help us with the repairs in this house.

b starting a new subject in school.

c being alone in a big noisy crowd.

d to help him with his homework.

e to learn.

f to see them at this type of restaurant.

g to visit this summer.

h watching TV.

B **Complete each sentence with the gerund or infinitive form of the verb in parentheses ( ).**

1 I spent a lot of time trying different sushi restaurants while I was in Japan. (try)
2 We had ______ about whether to buy their house or not. (think)
3 Sometimes it's hard ______ the only boy in the classroom. (be)
4 We needed someone ______ us a ride to the train station. (give)
5 I felt nervous ______ for the airplane to take off. (wait)
6 It's not unusual ______ more than you have. (want)
7 My car needs ______ fixed before I can drive it back home. (be)
8 There are sites that are interesting ______ in this ancient city. (visit)

3 GRAMMAR AND VOCABULARY

A **Circle the correct verb to complete the sentences. Then add another sentence using the cues in parentheses.**

1 A I spent time *to see* / *seeing* my sick grandmother this weekend. (make a difference)
B I think it really made a difference.
2 A I think I need a teacher *to talk* / *talking* about my future goals. (reassure)
B ______.
3 A I didn't waste my time *explaining* / *to explain* it to them. (value)
B ______.
4 A It's common *testing* / *to test* a product first before putting it on the market. (beneficial)
B ______.
5 A They always have volunteers *to help* / *helping* them during a crisis. (devote their life to)
B ______.
6 A The charity always needs more people *to support* / *supporting* them. One way to do this is to give money. (make a contribution)
B ______.

B **Use a gerund or infinitive to complete the sentences so that they are true for you.**

1 I take great pleasure in ______.
2 It's been beneficial ______.
3 There's a lot of use in ______.
4 I think it's worthwhile ______.
5 I get a lot of satisfaction out of ______.

7.2 BUYER'S REGRET

1 VOCABULARY: Making purchases

A **Circle the correct meaning for each sentence.**

1 I was silly to buy the expensive boots because I already have a closet full of them.
  (a) I regret the purchase.
  b I think the boots look ridiculous.

2 Our parents always help us to feel confident about doing things we don't think we can do.
  a Our parents convince us to do things.
  b Our parents encourage us to do things.

3 Mia has a lot of useful ideas that can help us solve these problems.
  a Mia's ideas are foolish.
  b Mia's ideas are practical.

4 My husband doesn't want me to buy the car because it is not a good value for the price.
  a He thinks the car is not worth the money.
  b He thinks the car does not have potential.

5 I hope the seminar will persuade you to sign up for French classes.
  a I hope the seminar will convince you.
  b I hope the seminar is practical.

6 Don't buy the cheapest shoes. They are not such good value.
  a I encouraged her to buy the cheapest shoes.
  b I urged her not to buy the cheapest shoes.

B **Complete the sentences with the words and phrases in the box.**

have appeal	have potential	look ridiculous
~~make financial sense~~	regretted the purchase	urged

1 It might ___make financial sense___ to buy this when it's on sale.
2 We should take these costumes off before leaving the party, so we don't ________ walking home.
3 Several lawyers strongly ________ the parents to take further legal action.
4 These regions ________ for economic development.
5 The commercials ________ which will attract a lot of people to their website.
6 Javier bought an expensive table. After he paid the delivery fee, he ________ .

C **THINK CRITICALLY** **What are some things that people may regret buying? Why might they regret their purchases?**

____

____

____

2 GRAMMAR: Infinitives after verbs with and without objects

A **Put the words in the correct order to make sentences.**

1 wanted / some of the repairs / she / to help / him / pay for / her

She wanted him to help her pay for some of the repairs.

2 encouraged / she / for my business / to buy / a new computer / me

____

3 on time / needed / Alejandra / the project / to finish

____

4 online / she / to buy / likes / clothes

____

5 to come / always / my parents / urged / on time / home / us

____

6 want / tomorrow morning / the children / to sleep in

____

7 to / decided / so / he / to talk / a doctor / was sick / my brother

____

8 to travel / at night / she / not / alone / us / warned

____

3 GRAMMAR AND VOCABULARY

A **Circle the correct infinitive and then write a phrase from exercises 1A and 1B to complete the conversation. Watch your verb tense.**

1 A My friend encouraged me *to wear* / *wear* an animal dress to the party.
B Oh, no. You must have looked ridiculous.

2 A We plan *waiting* / *to wait* on buying a house until the prices go down.
B Good idea. It ______________________________ .

3 A My boss is very upset because I forgot *to tell* / *telling* him I was going on vacation today.
B No wonder he's mad. That ______________________________ .

4 A I tend *wearing* / *to wear* comfortable shoes over fashionable ones.
B So, do I. I think it ______________________________ .

5 A I'm sad *to see* / *seeing* that it sold. I was hoping to buy it.
B Don't worry. It was ______________________________ .

6 A We decided *getting* / *to get* a new front door before we sell the house.
B That's a good idea. It will certainly ______________________________ .

7.3 A GOOD BARGAIN

1 LISTENING

A 7.01 **Listen to the conversation. Then write *T* (true) or *F* (false) next to the statements.**

1 Jorge doesn't want to accept Stella's first offer. ____
2 Stella thinks the rug is too expensive. ____
3 Stella doesn't buy the rug. ____

B 7.01 UNDERSTAND PERSUASIVE TECHNIQUES **Listen to the conversation again. Check (✓) the techniques each person uses to get the best deal.**

Stella says she loves the color of the rug ☐
says she only has $250 to buy the rug ☐
says the rug is too small ☐
says the rug is not worth that much ☐
says she's bought many rugs at street markets before ☐
tells Jorge she'll look around for another rug ☐

Jorge points out that many customers get a lot of satisfaction out of the rugs he sells ☐
tells Stella he made the rug himself ☐
refuses to give stuff for free ☐
reassures Stella that $250 is a good price for the rug ☐
says someone else will buy the rug if Stella doesn't ☐
says he'll clean the stain on the rug for Stella ☐

2 CRITICAL THINKING

A THINK CRITICALLY **Why do some people feel nervous about buying things at a street market? What are some advantages and disadvantages of buying things at a street market instead of a store?**

____

____

____

3 SPEAKING

A **Complete the conversations with the phrases in the box. You can use the phrases more than once. Then decide which conversation accepts an offer, and which rejects an offer.**

a little on the high side	don't think it's worth that much
go any lower	got a deal
~~how much are you asking for it~~	I can't accept that
the best I can do	throw in some stuff for free
sounds fair enough	sorry, but no deal
would you be willing to accept	

1 **A** I love this chair. So, [1] how much are you asking for it ?
B I'm selling it for $100.
A Oh, really? Hmmm. That's [2] ________ . Can you [3] ________ ?
B I can give it to you for $75.
A [4] ________ $60 for it?
B [5] ________ .
A Oh, that's too bad. I guess I'll have to shop somewhere else.

2 **A** Is this the car you're selling? So, [1] ________ ?
B I would like $5,000 for it.
A I'm sorry, but [2] ________ .
B I'll [3] ________ .
A Like what?
B A tank of gas and new windshield wipers.
A I'm sorry, but I [4] ________ .
B OK, $4,200 is [5] ________ .
A That [6] ________ .

B **Read the situation. Write a conversation that accepts an offer or refuses an offer between the buyer and the seller.**

Situation: Mario is on vacation at a beach resort. He is approached by a woman selling necklaces for $45 each. He really wants to buy one for his girlfriend, but he only wants to spend $30.

A [1] ________
B [2] ________
A [3] ________
B [4] ________
A [5] ________
B [6] ________

7.4 MONEY'S WORTH

1 READING

A IDENTIFY MAIN POINTS **Read the article. Check (✓) the best summary.**

a Spending money on yourself can increase happiness. ____

b Spending money on others can increase happiness. ____

c People who are wealthy should spend money on others. ____

SPENDING ON OTHERS COULD MAKE A DIFFERENCE IN YOUR LIFE

There's a Chinese saying that goes something like this: "If you want happiness for a day, do something for yourself. If you want happiness for a lifetime, do something for others." Many researchers believe these words of wisdom when it comes to how you spend money, once your basic needs are met, of course.

In related studies, researchers Elizabeth Dunn and Michael Norton noted in their book *Happy Money: The Science of Happier Spending* (2013) that people who spend their money on others seem to get more satisfaction than those who spend their money on themselves. Spending on those you care about, or even strangers, can boost overall happiness levels. But they do point out that happiness comes from spending money on others because you want to, not from spending it out of guilt or obligation.

In another study, the World Happiness Report (2019) revealed that there is a high level of unhappiness among Americans. It was reported that this could be due to people not spending enough of their money on others. Spending money on charities, or making donations, could make people happier. Just ask someone like Bill Gates. According to many, this billionaire is happy devoting his time and money to others. It's been said that he gets more pleasure in spending most of his billions on charities and scientific research than on personal luxuries.

The good news is you don't have to be wealthy to spend money on others. Buying someone a coffee, making a small contribution to a charity, or giving a few dollars to a homeless person could be worthwhile as it helps us communicate and connect with people. That warm, happy feeling you get every time you spend on others rather than on yourself might make a big difference to your level of happiness and overall well-being.

B IDENTIFY SUPPORTING DETAILS **Read the article again. Answer the questions.**

1 According to the article, what kind of spending makes people happier?

2 What do researchers Elizabeth Dunn and Michael Norton say about how to spend on others?

3 Why might many Americans be unhappy?

4 As mentioned in the article, what are some ways that we can spend money on others to make ourselves happier?

2 CRITICAL THINKING

A THINK CRITICALLY **Besides personal happiness, think of other reasons why spending money on others could be positive in someone's life. In what ways do you spend money on yourself? What about on others? How do you feel when you spend money on others?**

3 WRITING

A **Read part of an essay. What two arguments are given? What is the author's own opinion?**

Can Money Buy Happiness?

Recently, there have been a number of articles about what makes people happy. Many authors argue that having enough money to buy the necessary things in life can be enough for people to be happy, while others believe that those things might not be enough.

Let's consider some arguments in favor of how having enough money for the basic things in life can make people happy. To begin with, happiness can be achieved if we have money to pay for shelter, food, and clothing. When people are able to buy these things, they don't have to worry about their families or themselves. One thing for sure is that money can give us a sense of … . For example, money can … . Furthermore, money can help us feel healthy. For instance, … . Overall, these things in life can certainly help us feel happy.

On the other hand, having only enough money for the basic things in life might not always bring happiness. For some people, happiness comes from having things that make them more comfortable. For instance, having money beyond what we need might make certain people feel … . In addition, some people are happy having things such as … . These things can make their life seem more valuable. However, if people don't have things in life such as … , then what good is having money?

Money might not always buy happiness. It's my opinion that money can't always buy the things that truly are important to the quality of our lives. We can't buy our health or our friends … .

B **Read the essay again. Write ideas that could complete the essay.**

CHECK AND REVIEW

Read the statements. Can you do these things?

UNIT 7	Mark the boxes. ☑ I can do it. ? I am not sure. **I can …**	If you are not sure, go back to these pages in the Student's Book.
VOCABULARY	☐ **describe positive experiences.** ☐ **talk about making purchases.**	page 67 page 68
GRAMMAR	☐ **use gerunds and infinitives after adjectives, nouns, and pronouns.** ☐ **use infinitives after verbs with and without objects.**	page 67 page 69
LISTENING AND SPEAKING SKILLS	☐ **understand persuasive techniques.** ☐ **use arguments to accept and reject an offer.**	page 70 page 71
READING AND WRITING SKILLS	☐ **identify main ideas and supporting details.** ☐ **write a for-and-against essay.**	page 72 page 73

UNIT 8 SMALL THINGS MATTER

8.1 ANNOYING LITTLE THINGS

1 VOCABULARY: Describing neatness and messiness

A **Complete the sentences with the phrases in the box.**

arrange them neatly	disorganized	fold sth	hang sth up
jumbled up	leave things all over the place	line up	organized
put away	put sth in alphabetical order	~~put sth in a pile~~	
tangled up	throw something in/on		

1 When you ___put sth in a pile___, you position objects one on top of the other.

2 When you ______________________, especially paper or cloth, you bend it so that it takes up less room.

3 When you ______________________ shoes, you put them in a neat row.

4 When a cord is twisted in an untidy mass, it is ______________________.

5 When toys are mixed together untidily, they are ______________________.

6 When you ______________________ dishes, you put them where they are usually kept.

7 When you ______________________, you place it on a hanger or a hook.

8 When you ______________________, you arrange it in the same order as the letters of the alphabet.

9 When you put something quickly and carelessly on a chair, you ______________________ it.

10 When you plan things carefully and keep things tidy, you are ______________________.

11 When you put a group of objects in careful order, you ______________________.

12 When you are not good at planning or organizing things, you are ______________________.

13 When you ______________________, they are spread out in a large area in a disorganized way.

2 GRAMMAR: Modal-like expressions with *be*

A **Rewrite the sentences using the expressions in parentheses ().**

1 He is certain to be late because he cannot find his keys. (bound to)

He is bound to be late because he cannot find his keys.

2 He's going to meet his friends at the train station. (about to)

____

3 The train is expected to leave at 4:10 p.m. (supposed to)

____

4 His friends are certain to be mad if he misses the train. (sure to)

____

5 When he got there, he was made to go to another platform. (forced to)

____

B **Read the complaints that Tanya and Marco have about each other. Circle the correct modal to complete the sentences.**

It annoys me when I'm late for work. We are [1]*about to / supposed to* be at the train station at 8:00 a.m., but Tanya can never find her coat or shoes in the mornings. Since I don't want to be late again, I'm [2]*bound to / forced to* put everything near the front door after she goes to bed at night. It annoys me that when I get home her things are [3]*sure to / about to* be left all over the place again.

He should talk! When we are [4]*about to / sure to* leave in the morning, Marco always wants to wash the dishes first. We can never get to the train station on time. Sometimes, he's too organized. It really annoys me when I get home because he's [5]*supposed to / bound to* be cleaning and putting my things away.

C THINK CRITICALLY **Read the complaints again. Do you think it's reasonable for Tanya and Marco to be annoyed with each other? Give reasons why.**

____

____

____

D **Complete the sentences so that they are true for you.**

1 This week, I am due to _______________.

2 I was about to _______________, but _______________.

3 The weather is sure to be _______________ tomorrow.

4 When I was young, my parents forced me to _______________.

5 When I'm older, I'm bound to be _______________.

3 GRAMMAR AND VOCABULARY

A **Write sentences with your own ideas using the word prompts.**

1 forced to / leave things all over the place

When I was young, my mother was forced to pick up the toys we left all over the place.

2 bound to / throw on

_______________.

3 supposed to / put away

_______________.

4 sure to / put in alphabetical order

_______________.

5 about to / tangled up

_______________.

8.2 SIDE PROJECTS

1 VOCABULARY: Talking about progress

A **Circle the correct meaning of each vocabulary word or phrase.**

1 as expected	did not happen as predicted	happened as predicted
2 with ease	without problems	with problems
3 smoothly	easily	with difficulty
4 efficiently	slowly and badly	quickly and well
5 little by little	slowly and gradually	quickly and rapidly
6 with difficulty	without problems	with problems
7 in my own time	when I am not working	when I am working
8 steadily	rapidly	gradually
9 successfully	achieving good results	achieving bad results
10 thoroughly	quickly	completely
11 at my own pace	at a speed comfortable to you	to do something slowly
12 effectively	with no results	with good results

B **Complete the sentences with words or phrases from exercise 1A.**

1 We can't repair our house all at once, so we'll have to repair it little by little.
2 ______________, he was late again for the meeting. He's always late.
3 If all goes ______________, we should arrive by nine o'clock.
4 I ______________ enjoyed the performance tonight.
5 The medicine works more ______________ if you take a hot drink after it.
6 Jorge finally finished his essay, but ______________.
7 She wasn't in any pain and won the 400-meter race ______________.
8 I like to make and sell wooden chairs ______________ in the evenings and at weekends.
9 They are so organized. They run their business very ______________.
10 A number of patients have been treated ______________ with the new drug.
11 Food prices have risen ______________ over the years.
12 I studied English ______________ at home. It was slower than taking classes, but less expensive.

2 GRAMMAR: Future forms

A **Underline the verb phrase in each sentence that shows the future.**

1. Eventually, we'll be living in our newly built home.
2. I don't think she's going to attend the event.
3. Sooner or later, she might want to go back to her home country.
4. In a few years, we'll be buying a new car.
5. This book won't fill you with joy, but it will give you some inspiration.
6. If my business doesn't run efficiently, I might hire more people.
7. I'm not going to her party unless she invites me herself.
8. This side project of mine is going to allow me to make some extra money.

B **Correct the mistake in each sentence.**

1. Next month, we're going ~~moving~~ to another area in the city. *to move*
2. She'll be return from her trip very soon. ______
3. Eating too much candy won't be killing you, but it will hurt your teeth. ______
4. When you get there, you go to take the bus to their house. ______
5. Next week, we're going to be travel in Europe. ______
6. By the summer, they won't be make any more money from these hats. ______
7. I guess you will be feel tired after working in the sun all day. ______
8. This presentation is going take a long time, so let's get comfortable. ______

3 GRAMMAR AND VOCABULARY

A **Create sentences in the future form with your own ideas.**

1. as expected / technology in the future
   As expected, technology in the future will be changing all the time.
2. successfully / a side project
   ______.
3. efficiently and effectively / my business
   ______.
4. little by little / my future plans
   ______.
5. in my own time / learn a new language
   ______.
6. smoothly / getting more customers
   ______.

B **THINK CRITICALLY** **What are the pros of turning a side project into a business? What might be the cons?**

______

8.3 THE LITTLE TOUCHES

1 LISTENING

A 8.01 **Listen to the conversation between two siblings, Sarah and Leo. Check (✓) the "little touches" they are planning for their grandma's birthday.**

- Bake her a cake ☐
- Order pink balloons ☐
- Order food from her favorite Greek restaurant ☐
- Buy fancy napkins ☐
- Have a fun theme ☐
- Get a karaoke machine ☐
- Play her favorite songs ☐
- Tell people to dress like they did in the 50s ☐

B 8.01 RECOGNIZE EMPHASIS **Listen to the conversation again and underline the words which are emphasized. Write *C* for the words that show a contrasting idea.**

1 I think we need to do something <u>really</u> special. ______
2 Hmmm, I'm not sure she would like that. ______
3 That's such a terrific idea! ______
4 Of course, I bet everyone will love that! ______
5 My house is such a mess. ______
6 How about we throw the surprise party in your apartment? ______
7 What a fabulous idea! ______
8 She likes the new Greek restaurant. ______
9 Grandma will be so happy. ______
10 Don't worry. It will. ______
11 That's such an awesome idea! ______

2 CRITICAL THINKING

A THINK CRITICALLY **How might choosing a theme for a party or an event help make planning it easier? How might having a theme make it difficult to plan?**

____
____
____
____
____
____
____
____
____
____

3 SPEAKING

A **Circle the correct words to complete the conversations.**

1 **A** What should we do for Sandra's retirement party? She's worked here for almost 20 years!

B Going out for lunch always [1](goes / *went*) over well for retirement parties.

A Hmmm, I don't think that's a good way to [2](*have / approach*) it. One [3](*thing / way*) we could do is have it catered.

B I [4](*know / bet*) everyone will love that!

2 **A** What should we do for Dunia's graduation? She's worked so hard to become a lawyer.

B It never [1](*hurts / goes*) to give her money.

A Hmmm. Or another [2](*idea / thing*) we could do is take her on a vacation.

B That's always [3](*good / worth*) considering.

3 **A** What should we do for John's birthday? He'll be turning 12 years old!

B One [1](*approach / thing*) we could do is take him to a movie.

A Hmmm, I don't think that's a good way to [2](*consider / approach*) it. Having a party always [3](*goes / went*) over well.

B That's such an awesome [4](*idea / approach*)!

B **Choose an idea for an event from the list below. Write a conversation between you and a friend who is helping you plan the event.**

- A dinner party to congratulate your husband on his big job promotion
- A going away party for your friends who are taking a trip around the world
- A New Year's Eve party
- A housewarming party to celebrate moving into your new house

A ______________________________

B ______________________________

A ______________________________

B ______________________________

8.4 A SMILE GOES A LONG WAY

1 READING

A **IDENTIFY WRITER'S PURPOSE** **Read the article. What's its purpose? Check (✓) the best statement.**

a To tell readers to be calm when they are in traffic. _____

b To advise readers why they shouldn't worry and complain about the small stuff. _____

c To warn readers that feeling stressed can weaken the immune system. _____

HOW DO YOU DEAL WITH THE LITTLE THINGS IN LIFE?

Are you one of those people who complain and worry about the small stuff? Well, don't. Scientists have recently discovered that people who worry and complain about the little annoyances in life may be putting their health at risk.

While there are some people who get through the small stuff—heavy traffic, miserable weather, or canceled dinner plans—with ease, there are those who react with anger or frustration. When these little challenges or difficulties arise, emotions are bound to rise, too. Our bodies react, but not in a good way.

Recent studies show that negative emotions can flood the bloodstream with stress hormones. These hormones are released into the body when it interprets danger or threat. When they do, it can decrease our energy levels, increase heart rate and blood pressure, and in some instances, slow down digestion and reproduction organs. If that's not enough, stress hormones can make the immune system weak, which can cause other illnesses in the body.

What can we do? Well, practice being calm. Meditate, find deep breathing exercises, or concentrate on happy, positive thoughts when things don't go smoothly. Visualize the road becoming free of traffic or that rainy day bringing sunshine. Calming the mind and imagining things will work out can improve our health, both physically and mentally.

It takes practice to be calm. But we need to train our brain to deal with strong emotions when something annoys or frustrates us. So, the next time something small irritates you, learn from it and take control of your reaction. Know that worrying over the little stuff will not only ruin your day, but will be sure to affect your health, too.

B **Read the article again. What specific examples of why we shouldn't complain about the small stuff does the writer mention? What advice does the writer suggest?**

2 CRITICAL THINKING

A **THINK CRITICALLY** **What situations might make people worry and complain about the "big stuff"? Think of three examples. Why might they worry about these things?**

_____

_____

_____

3 WRITING

A **Read the complaint email. Underline the problem and how Mira would like the company to solve it.**

Reply Forward

To: Ms. Suzanne Castillo
From: Mira Kim

Dear Ms. Castillo,

I recently bought a $450 printer from your company. I made the purchase on December 17 and the receipt number is 294738. It was a present for my husband who needed a high-quality laser printer for his new business. However, this product is definitely not high-quality. When the printer was delivered, the box was damaged and the paper tray was broken. Also, the glass is scratched, so any copies that we make have lines on them. Finally, the printer is very slow. This is unacceptable and I would like a replacement printer.

I have attached a copy of my receipt to this email. I would like your company to collect the broken printer from my house and deliver a new one as soon as possible. I look forward to hearing from you in the next week.

Sincerely,
Mira Kim

B **Read the email again. Choose an idea below and write a more polite email that describes the problem and how you would like the company to solve it. Use expressions like *I find*, *I feel*, *I believe*, or *I think* if you can.**

The couch you ordered is wobbly and uncomfortable.
Your car is still making a loud noise after it was repaired by a mechanic.
The hotel room was small and dirty.

CHECK AND REVIEW

Read the statements. Can you do these things?

UNIT 8	Mark the boxes. ☑ I can do it. ? I am not sure. **I can …**	If you are not sure, go back to these pages in the Student's Book.
VOCABULARY	☐ **talk about neatness and messiness.** ☐ **talk about progress.**	page 76 page 78
GRAMMAR	☐ **use modal-like expressions with *be*.** ☐ **use future forms.**	page 77 page 79
LISTENING AND SPEAKING SKILLS	☐ **recognize emphasis.** ☐ **suggest and show interest in ideas.**	page 80 page 81
READING AND WRITING SKILLS	☐ **identify the writer's purpose.** ☐ **write a complaint letter.**	page 82 page 83

UNIT 9 THINGS HAPPEN

9.1 TURNING POINTS

1 VOCABULARY: Luck and choice

A **Circle the correct word or phrase in each sentence.**

1 Finding work was difficult for Greg, but he finally got a *lucky break* / *chance encounter* with this company.
2 Samuel was *in the right place at the right time* / *wound up* because he found a good parking spot.
3 Little did I know that she would *wind up* / *not believe my luck* as my next manager.
4 She was *deliberate decision* / *fortunate* to be cheerful at work.
5 Is it just a *coincidence* / *chance encounter* that the person who ran the contest won first prize?
6 Mariana went through a *life-changing experience* / *lucky break* when she survived the accident.
7 You can't help but admire her *fortunate* / *determination* to reach her goal.
8 We made a *lucky break* / *deliberate decision* to spend less money on things we don't need.
9 The *path* / *fate* to success is not without difficulty.
10 They believed that *fate* / *deliberate decision* brought them together.
11 I couldn't *be fortunate* / *believe my luck* when I saw I had won the prize.
12 He didn't expect to meet his wife through a *coincidence* / *chance encounter* at a café.

B **Imagine you are in these situations. What might you think? Complete the sentences with words from exercise 1A.**

1 You met a movie star in the elevator on your way down to the lobby.
I was in the ___right___ place at the right time.
2 You found someone to help you sell your car.
It was very ________ I had him to help me.
3 You saw an old friend getting on the same plane as you.
It was a ________ that we were on the same plane.
4 You got a job with that big company right after you graduated.
It was a ________ that I got this great job so quickly.
5 You missed the bus so you wouldn't have to go to the meeting.
I made a ________ decision to miss the bus.
6 You studied the lines for weeks to get the acting part.
I had a lot of ________ to get this part.

2 GRAMMAR: Unreal conditionals

A **Put the words in the correct order to make sentences.**

1 would've shopped / I / expensive / if / somewhere else / expensive / knew / I / it was going to be

If I knew it was going to be expensive, I would've shopped somewhere else .

2 study / would've failed the exam / if / I / hadn't helped me / I / he

______________________________.

______________________________.

3 would help / if / could / I / you / I

______________________________.

______________________________.

4 the Great Wall of China / I / if / anywhere in the world / could go / go see / I'd

______________________________.

______________________________.

5 all the cake / she'd / if / could reach the table / eat / our dog

______________________________.

______________________________.

6 Tamara might've gotten the job / if / hadn't been late / she

______________________________.

______________________________.

B **Circle the correct words to complete the sentences.**

1 If I'd known you were allergic to nuts, I ______ an apple pie.

a would make (b) would've made

2 If I hadn't ______ him when I did, I might not have become a dentist.

a have met b met

3 If you ______ a good friend, you'd help him with his exam.

a were b are

4 If Clara ______ busy, she might not have missed the call.

a weren't b hadn't been

5 I ______ figured this out if I hadn't read the instructions.

a couldn't b couldn't have

6 If the book had more action, I ______ be interested in reading it.

a would b will

3 GRAMMAR AND VOCABULARY

A **Use your own ideas to complete the unreal conditional sentences.**

1 I was fortunate. If I hadn't had met her, I *wouldn't have gone travelling* .

2 Fate is what brought those two together. If she ______________________________, she might not have ______________________________.

3 If she ______________________________, she'd be on a much better path then the one she's on now.

4 If I ______________________________, I'd have more determination to finish this project.

5 It was a coincidence. If Andres ______________________________, he wouldn't ______________________________.

9.2 WHY DID I DO IT?

1 VOCABULARY: Commenting on mistakes

A **Find words in the word search.**

h	a	r	d	b	c	h	j	u	i	b
u	a	b	z	k	j	l	c	o	n	a
r	c	u	f	l	w	b	m	p	c	w
r	v	d	k	i	a	s	n	k	o	k
y	e	j	y	t	t	i	m	i	m	w
d	u	m	b	s	c	l	d	c	p	a
h	f	o	g	e	h	l	o	k	e	r
i	w	v	w	q	r	y	t	p	t	d
x	g	e	h	f	a	u	l	t	e	q
f	u	n	n	y	w	c	u	s	n	r
u	n	f	o	r	t	u	n	a	t	e

awkward
fault
hard
incompetent
move
unfortunate
dumb
funny side
hurry
kick yourself
~~silly~~
watch

B **Complete the sentences with words from exercise 1A.**

1 She showed little thought and judgment when she did that. It was a/an silly mistake.
2 You are going to spill the milk if you don't ________ what you're doing.
3 Slow down. You're in too much of a/an ________ and you might make a mistake.
4 She found herself in a/an ________ situation when she forgot his name.
5 It's your own ________ that you lost your phone.
6 Lucky for me, he saw the ________ side of my error.
7 I learned the ________ way that going to school and working at the same time is challenging.
8 You know you'll ________ yourself if you forget to do it, so just do it now!
9 It was a bad ________ on my part for getting involved.
10 I know you need the money, but I think selling your favorite watch is a/an ________ thing to do.
11 She described him as being totally ________ at his job. He wasn't able to do the simplest task.
12 It was ________ that it rained during their game.

2 GRAMMAR: Wishes and regrets

A **Circle the correct words or phrases to complete the sentences. Then write if the sentences express present or past wishes.**

1 If only I *could* / *can* play the piano! present
2 I wish I *taught* / *was teaching* in that other school again. ______
3 I wish she *attends* / *had attended* the meeting. ______
4 If only they *have* / *had* been more careful. ______
5 I wish you *could* / *can* see the movie with us. ______
6 If only someone *had taught* / *was teaching* me this when I was younger. ______
7 I wish I *talked* / *had talked* to her yesterday. ______
8 I wish I *was going* / *can go* on vacation with them. ______

B **Complete the sentences with the correct form of the verbs in the box.**

go	grow	have	know	leave	perform	stop	~~study~~

1 I wish that I wasn't studying art history.
2 If only someone had ______ her from getting up on the stage and embarrassing herself.
3 I wish I had ______ a little sister when I was growing up.
4 Tomas wishes he could ______ vegetables in his garden, but it is too small.
5 If only I ______ how to use a computer, I'd be doing a different job.
6 If only he ______ the house earlier, he wouldn't be stuck in a traffic jam.
7 I wish I could ______ on vacation with you next week, but I'm busy.
8 Amelia wishes she was ______ in the school play this year.

3 GRAMMAR AND VOCABULARY

A **For each conversation, comment on mistakes using the phrase in parentheses. Then finish each response with a wish or regret.**

1 **A** I made a big mistake yesterday when I quit my job.
B That was a bad move. (be a bad move)
A You're right. I wish I hadn't quit my job.

2 **A** I need to rush, or I'll be in trouble for being late.
B ______. (be your own fault)
A You're right. If only my boss ______.

3 **A** I think I'm going to demand a big pay raise.
B ______. (be a dumb thing to do)
A You're right. I wish I ______.

4 **A** I couldn't find my train ticket, so I had to buy another one.
B ______. (be unfortunate)
A I know. If only I ______.

5 **A** He needs more training. He cannot do what I ask him to do.
B ______. (be incompetent)
A You're right. I wish he ______.

6 **A** It was difficult starting my own business because I didn't get any help.
B I bet ______. (learn sth the hard way)
A You're right. If only I ______.

9.3 MY MISTAKE

1 LISTENING

A 9.01 **Listen to the conversation. Then write *T* (true) or *F* (false) next to the statements.**

1 Henry has an audition today. F
2 Carmen made a lot of silly mistakes. ______
3 Laura Medford was in a different room. ______
4 Carmen tells Henry to leave his phone at home or in his car. ______
5 Laura Medford showed up at the office. ______
6 Henry didn't notice Laura Medford at the coffee shop. ______
7 Laura Medford spilled coffee all over the front of Henry's expensive pants. ______
8 Henry was told to come and do the audition again. ______

B 9.01 IDENTIFY FEELINGS **Listen to the conversation again. Circle the word that best describes Henry's feelings.**

1 When Henry said his lines in front of his favorite actress, he felt …
a cheerful **b** confused **c** calm
2 When his phone rang in the middle of the audition, he was …
a amused **b** sad **c** annoyed
3 When Henry saw Laura Medford at the coffee shop, he was …
a surprised **b** calm **c** angry
4 When Laura spilled coffee all over his expensive shirt, Henry was …
a confused **b** annoyed **c** calm
5 When he was told to come and do the audition again, he felt …
a cheerful **b** annoyed **c** amused

2 CRITICAL THINKING

A THINK CRITICALLY **Why do you think it would be hard for some people to accept their mistakes? Think of how they might feel or what they might fear.**

____
____
____
____
____

3 SPEAKING

A **(Circle) the correct word to complete the expressions of reassurances.**

1 **A** Look at my hair. It's a mess!
B It's not that *good* / (*bad*).

2 **A** I think I left my wallet on the table at the café.
B We all make *mistakes* / *errors*.

3 **A** I didn't get the promotion I was expecting at work.
B That's the way it *went* / *goes*.

4 **A** I'm upset that I broke my arm in the car accident last weekend.
B It could have been *worse* / *better*.

5 **A** The vase broke when I accidentally dropped it.
B You're not the only one who's *done* / *did* that.

6 **A** I'm so embarrassed that I forgot her birthday.
B Don't worry. No one is *good* / *perfect*.

7 **A** If I don't find a job soon, I'll have to move out of this apartment.
B It'll turn out all *wrong* / *right*.

8 **A** Well, it's done now. I can't go back and re-write the test.
B You're right. There's no use in *crying* / *laughing* over spilled milk.

9 **A** I don't think they're going to call me back for a second interview.
B What are you worrying *for* / *over*? It will be fine.

B **For each situation write an expression of reassurance and then give advice.**

1 **A** Oh, no. I got a terrible haircut!
B It's not that bad. It'll grow out soon.

2 **A** I lost one of the books I borrowed from my friend.
B ______________________

3 **A** I feel so bad. I won't be able to make it to her party this weekend.
B ______________________

4 **A** I failed my driving test.
B ______________________

5 **A** I couldn't get tickets to the big concert this weekend.
B ______________________

6 **A** I'm sorry, but I got the schedule all wrong. I think we missed the train.
B ______________________

9.4 GOOD CONVERSATIONS

1 READING

A **MAKE PREDICTIONS** **Read the title of the article. What do you think the writer means by "conversation flow"? Then read the article. Was your prediction correct?**

HOME NEWS BLOG SIGN IN

THE SECRET OF CONVERSATION FLOW

What makes conversations so special? Well, they all have something called *conversation flow*. Conversation flow happens when conversation is comfortable, effortless, and smooth. It's the way conversations are supposed to work.

Sometimes, conversation flow seems to happen automatically. You and your conversation partner get along and the conversation feels very friendly and natural. That's great when it happens, but what do you do when the conversation doesn't flow?

That's where the ideas of invitation and inspiration come in. An invitation is when you say something that lets your conversation partner clearly know it's her turn to speak. And when your partner says something to you that makes you want to speak, that's known as inspiration. Invitation and inspiration are the key ingredients of smooth, comfortable conversation. These conversational strategies keep the conversation flowing. Learn how to use them and you will have conversations free of awkward pauses and fake small talk.

Here's how it works:
Let's say that you and your friend Steve are chatting as you work.
You ask, "How was your weekend?"
Steve replies, "Oh, it was great. How was yours?"
You reply, "It was fine."
Steve says nothing and goes back to work.

What happened? Well, you didn't give Steve a clear invitation or a strong inspiration. Without either of those things, he didn't know what to say next (and perhaps was unsure if it was his turn to speak). So, he didn't respond. The conversation failed.

Without an invitation or an inspiration, your partner might not know what to say or whether to respond. That's why you want to make sure to offer invitations and inspirations to your partner in order to have a conversation flow.

B **Read the article again. How do invitation and inspiration keep a conversation flowing? What is an example of an invitation you could give Steve to keep the conversation going?**

2 CRITICAL THINKING

A **THINK CRITICALLY** **Do you know anyone who is good at conversation? What kind of things do they talk about, and what conversational strategies do they use?**

3 WRITING

A Read the article. Summarize the tips it gives. What is the easiest tip to do in the article? What about the hardest?

HOW TO START A CONVERSATION WITH THREE BODY LANGUAGE TIPS

BODY LANGUAGE TIPS

Using body language to help you start a conversation can lead to great conversation. You do not have to say much because just a look or a movement can be beneficial.

The following shows the main points of body language you should be aware of when you want to start a conversation.

EYE USE:

We can learn all about a person through their eyes. Your eyes can say many things and sometimes you may be unaware of what your eyes are saying. Be careful not to let your eyes say you are bored and are not listening.

BODY MOVES:

The way you move your hands, arms, feet, and head can say many things. Crossing your arms, tapping your foot rapidly, or putting your hands on your hips can all say things that might seem negative. Always be aware of what your body is saying.

FACIAL EXPRESSIONS:

Smiling can say more than words so be aware of your facial expressions at all times. You may frown and be unaware of it. Facial expressions can often be misunderstood if you give someone a serious look. They may think you do not like them.

Just make sure you are using the rest of your body to speak as well, and your facial expressions should come across clearly. Your eyes, body, and face can carry on a whole conversation for you.

B **Read the article again. Think of tips or go online for ideas about how to end a conversation. Write an article that gives at least three tips. Include a title, headings for each tip, and advice / explanations under each heading. Remember to use parallel structure in lists.**

CHECK AND REVIEW

Read the statements. Can you do these things?

UNIT 9	Mark the boxes. ☑ I can do it. ? I am not sure. **I can …**	If you are not sure, go back to these pages in the Student's Book.
VOCABULARY	☐ use expressions for luck and choice. ☐ talk about mistakes.	page 86 page 89
GRAMMAR	☐ use unreal conditionals. ☐ describe wishes and regrets.	page 87 page 89
LISTENING AND SPEAKING SKILLS	☐ reassure someone about a problem. ☐ use expressions of reassurance correctly.	page 90 page 91
READING AND WRITING SKILLS	☐ make predictions. ☐ write an article giving tips.	page 92 page 93

10.1 ARE WE UNIQUE?

1 VOCABULARY: Describing characteristics

A **Complete the sentences with the words in the box.**

build	characteristic	feature
female	gender	individual
likeness	look	look-alike
male	~~match~~	similarity

1 He was a perfect ___match___ to Luisa's outgoing personality.
2 A big nose is a typical ______ in her family.
3 They have the same ______ . Their hair is very similar and so are their clothes.
4 It's more important to be a/an ______ than to copy everyone else.
5 Does this test show the ______ of the baby?
6 Her favorite ______ has always been her thick and curly hair.
7 I can see the ______ between you and your father.
8 She was voted the best ______ country singer in the world.
9 She has a slim ______ just like her mother.
10 Jorge is a twenty-five-year old ______ with dark hair and blue eyes.
11 When I look at you, there's a definite family ______ around the eyes.
12 She's a Marilyn Monroe ______ with her blond hair and pretty smile.

B **Answer the questions with your own information.**

1 What kind of look did you have when you were younger?

______

2 What are some of your family's characteristics?

______

3 Have you ever been told you're a look-alike for someone famous? If so, who?

______

4 What is your favorite feature? What is your least favorite?

______

C **THINK CRITICALLY What are some common reasons people change their facial features to avoid looking older? Do you think this is a good idea? Why or why not?**

______

______

______

______

2 GRAMMAR: Gerunds after prepositions

A **Complete the sentences with the correct form of the verbs in the box. Then underline the verb and the preposition.**

~~build~~	exercise	go	have
pay	understand	wear	win

1 We plan on ___building___ a new addition at the back of our house.
2 I often wonder about the possibility of ______ back to school.
3 She was concerned about ______ surgery next week.
4 Antonio and his wife did not like the idea of ______ the extra fee.
5 He's always succeeded in ______ games of chess.
6 Have you thought about ______ a watch? You're always losing track of time.
7 What are the benefits of ______ daily?
8 The experiment resulted in ______ more about the cancer drug.

B **Rewrite the sentences by putting the verbs in parentheses in the correct place.**

1 He succeeded in more about his team. (learn)
He succeeded in learning more about his team.

2 What are the risks of eights cups of coffee a day? (drink)

3 We really like the idea of him to visit us this summer. (come)

4 Martha and her husband were concerned about home in the heavy rain. (drive)

5 Christopher wondered about the possibility of a long vacation. (take)

6 We plan on this project by the end of the week. (finish)

3 GRAMMAR AND VOCABULARY

A **Complete the sentences with a gerund and your own ideas.**

1 I never plan on ______ my facial features because ______.
2 I sometimes think about ______ my look so I can ______.
3 The risks of ______ to change your build are ______.
4 The idea of ______ a look-alike somewhere in the world is ______.
5 Some benefits of ______ a female might be ______.

10.2 YOU, THE CUSTOMER

1 VOCABULARY: Describing research

A **Complete the sentences with one of the word pairs from the box. Write *N* (noun) or *V* (verb) to show how each word is used in the sentence.**

analyze/analysis	assess/assessment	calculate/calculation	demonstrate/demonstration
~~examine/examination~~	identify/identification	survey/survey	

1 **a** They need to ___examine___ the chemical content in the metal. ___V___
  b Once the data is collected, there will be a/an ___examination___ of it. ___N___
2 **a** Let me give you a/an ______ on how this works. ______
  b He wanted to ______ to her how it works. ______
3 **a** They had to show their ______ before entering the building. ______
  b The research will be used to ______ training needs. ______
4 **a** They collect the data and ______ the store profits. ______
  b If their ______ is wrong, they have to collect new data. ______
5 **a** It's too early to ______ if the product will be successful. ______
  b Her ______ of the production cost was completely inaccurate. ______
6 **a** A recent ______ showed that teenagers prefer to shop online. ______
  b The researchers had to ______ two age groups for their report. ______
7 **a** Simon's team had to ______ ways to re-route heavy traffic. ______
  b This part of the project still needs a complete ______ . ______

2 GRAMMAR: Causative verbs

A **Complete the sentences with the correct form of the verb in parentheses.**

1 Working at night allows him ___to go___ (go) to school during the day.
2 The school lets parents ________ (know) if their child needs help.
3 You need to protect your identity from ________ (be) stolen online.
4 Computerization should enable them ________ (reduce) staffing costs.
5 If you wait here, we will have someone ________ (collect) it for you.
6 A system failure can cause everyone ________ (panic).
7 It's important to keep this information from ________ (reach) your senior staff.
8 Our manager sometimes makes us ________ (stay) late on the weekends.
9 Unfortunately, her sprained ankle prevents her from ________ (drive).
10 They put up barriers on the highway to stop cars from ________ (enter).

B **Check (✓) the correct sentences. Correct the incorrect sentences.**

1 Online shopping allows people ~~having~~ to have more time to themselves. ☐
2 Security guards prevent people from stealing items from the store. ✓
3 Having a good marketing strategy causes people wanting to buy more. ☐
4 Something must be done to stop them from arguing. ☐
5 Is this something they make all employees doing after their training? ☐
6 The new procedure has everyone to sign in first before their shift. ☐
7 The phone app lets you to know how much you have spent in the store. ☐
8 Georgina's shoes enabled her walking comfortably around the mall. ☐

3 GRAMMAR AND VOCABULARY

A **Circle the correct word and then complete the sentences with your own ideas.**

1 When people *calculate* / *calculation* their yearly budgets, it keeps ___them from spending too much money___.
2 *Analyzing* / *analysis* shopping trends allows ________.
3 Using fake *identify* / *identification* can prevent ________.
4 *Demonstrate* / *demonstrating* a new product on TV lets ________.
5 Industry *surveys* / *survey* enables ________.
6 *Assess* / *assessing* a product and its reviews makes ________.
7 The *examine* / *examination* of people selling their products online has stopped some ________.

10.3 A CAREFUL CHOICE

1 LISTENING

A 10.01 **Listen to Anton talk about two jobs. What are they? How does he feel about them?**

B 10.01 LISTEN FOR CONTRASTING IDEAS **Listen to the conversation again. Are Anton's ideas about the research company (R) or the sales company (S)? Which job does he like most? Which job would you choose?**

1 Everyone looked happy there. S

2 The work is similar to my current job. ______

3 I'll be able to walk to work. ______

4 I can make good money. ______

5 I'd be responsible for a lot of the research. ______

6 I'd use my sales skills. ______

7 The pay isn't great. ______

8 It'll be long hours. ______

9 I'll learn more. ______

2 CRITICAL THINKING

A THINK CRITICALLY **How can you tell by looking at a company online that it would be a good place to work? Think of three important things that you would look for.**

3 SPEAKING

A **Complete the phrases with a word in the box.**

far	funny	gut	hunch
~~impression~~	judging	see	strikes

1 A You look happy today.
  B I get the ___impression___ that everything went well at the meeting last night.

2 A Sandra still hasn't shown up to work.
  B I have a ______________ feeling that she might not come in at all.

3 A Michael doesn't seem himself lately.
  B I have a ______________ that he's going to quit soon.

4 A She left a big mess in the kitchen this morning.
  B ______________ by appearance, she must've been in a rush.

5 A Their house is so big!
  B What ______________ me about their house is that even though it's big, it still feels cozy.

6 A It's dark and there are no cars parked outside.
  B As ______________ as I can tell, the restaurant is closed.

7 A She looks good in that dress.
  B From what I can ______________ , she's on a new diet.

8 A The technology company is doing very well.
  B My ______________ feeling is that more people will apply to work here.

B **Look at the photos. Give your impressions about the two places. Use some of the expressions from exercise 3A.**

1

Restaurant 1

1 ______________

Restaurant 2

2 ______________

2

Beach 1

1 ______________

Beach 2

2 ______________

3

Workplace 1

1 ______________

Workplace 2

2 ______________

10.4 A PROFESSIONAL PROFILE

1 READING

A How can a company make more money with a professional profile? Read the article. Were your ideas the same as those in the article?

WRITE A COMPANY PROFILE THAT WINS BUSINESS

An attractive company profile is a great way to get potential customers to buy from you. Here are a few tips that will help you write the perfect profile.

1. **Think about what customers want to know and adjust your content accordingly**
   Content is often based on what the company thinks their potential clients want to know. Before you prepare your document, you need to understand exactly what your potential clients would want to know about you.

2. **Gather feedback**
   If you don't have a company profile, talk to the clients you already have, your friends, or your family. Ask them what questions they have about your products or services and try to provide the answers when you create the profile.

3. **Update your current profile**
   If you already have a company profile, ask a few clients for their honest feedback on it. Think about the questions you are most frequently asked by your customers. These questions point to issues you'll need to address when you update your profile.

4. **Use images**
   A lot of companies don't use images in their company profile, and this is a missed opportunity. If you're including information on the business owner and staff members, put photos next to their profiles. This helps to build a connection between the company and the client. You may also consider including a photo of your building or office.

5. **Strengthen your brand**
   A company profile can be used to outline and reinforce what your business is about and establish your identity in the marketplace. Don't forget to use your logo and company colors. This will ensure that your customers will always know who you are. It also makes your profile look more professional.

B **TAKE NOTES** Read the article again. Take notes about each of the five points. Then summarize each point with a sentence.

2 CRITICAL THINKING

A **THINK CRITICALLY** Imagine you're a small business owner. If you want to win more business, what questions would you ask your customers?

3 WRITING

A **Read an excerpt from a company profile. Underline the language that is too informal. Is there any language that is considered too formal?**

COMPANY PROFILE

Write Design is a self-publishing company for the young and old, and everyone in between! Write Design makes it super easy for you to design, publish, and promote your book. You can probably sell a lot of the professional-quality printed books and eBooks that we will make for you.

WD was founded by Liza Demetria in 2012. She is an author herself. She is working with a team of designers and media experts who share a passion for helping people bring their stories to life. Write Design authors have created a ton of books using their collection of book-making tools. A new book is created almost every minute! They are based in New York with offices in London …

B **USE PROFESSIONAL LANGUAGE Write a better version of the company profile in exercise A using more professional language. Add more details using ideas from the box or some of your own.**

- She has over 10 years of publishing experience.
- She has worked for one of the biggest publishing companies in the world.
- She started writing at the age of five and learned from her grandmother who wrote a bestseller.
- She knows how tough the publishing industry is.
- Millions of Write Designs books have been sold on Amazon.
- Books are her business.

CHECK AND REVIEW

Read the statements. Can you do these things?

UNIT 10	Mark the boxes. ✔ I can do it. ? I am not sure. **I can …**	If you are not sure, go back to these pages in the Student's Book.
VOCABULARY	☐ **people's characteristics.** ☐ **customer research.**	page 98 page 100
GRAMMAR	☐ **use gerunds after prepositions.** ☐ **use complements of verbs describing cause and effect.**	page 99 page 101
LISTENING AND SPEAKING SKILLS	☐ **listen for contrasting ideas.** ☐ **give your impressions.**	page 102 page 103
READING AND WRITING SKILLS	☐ **take notes.** ☐ **write a professional profile.**	page 104 page 105

UNIT 11 REALLY?

11.1 FAKE!

1 VOCABULARY: Describing consumer goods

A **Circle the correct meaning of each vocabulary word.**

1 fake
   (a) an object that is made to look real or valuable — b an object that is real or valuable
2 genuine
   a real, exactly what it appears to be — b not real, not what it appears to be
3 imperfect
   a in perfect condition — b damaged, has problems
4 authentic
   a real, true, or what people say it is — b not real, false, not what people say it is
5 legal
   a not allowed by the law — b allowed by the law
6 deadly
   a likely to cause death — b unlikely to cause death
7 fireproof
   a able to be damaged by fire — b unable to be damaged by fire
8 illegal
   a allowed by the law — b not allowed by the law
9 sophisticated
   a made in a complicated way — b made in an uncomplicated way
10 counterfeit
   a made to look like the real thing — b made to look better than the real thing
11 original
   a related to a first or real product — b related to copies of a real product
12 second-rate
   a cheaply made — b well made
13 inferior
   a not as good as something else — b just as good as something else

2 GRAMMAR: Passive forms

A **Underline the passive form in each sentence.**

1 These watches are not always made of quality material.
2 It's unlikely that the company will be stopped from producing these cheap products.
3 Two pink handbags were sold in the store last week.
4 Counterfeit watches were discovered while they were being sold on the streets.
5 Nothing is going to be sold by the athletic company this year.
6 The original painting was created by Sergio.

B **Rewrite the sentences using the correct form of the verbs in parentheses.**

1 The shoes *are made* by a small, Italian company. (make)
2 Our house ______ by a professional company next year. (renovate)
3 The little dog ______ in her oversized handbag. No one saw it. (carry)
4 Instructions ______ to you in the next few days. (sent)
5 The operation was a success. All the counterfeit money ______ by the police. (collect)
6 Illegal copies of the movies ______ by many of the stores. (sell)
7 The store is closing. Everything ______ at half price.(sell)
8 The problem is that second-rate items ______ to last long. (not design)

3 GRAMMAR AND VOCABULARY

A **Complete the sentences with your own ideas. Use passive forms.**

1 The genuine leather shoes *were being sold at a much higher price*.
2 Delicious food ______ at the authentic Italian restaurant.
3 Deadly chemicals ______ to make the jeans.
4 Sophisticated counterfeits ______ all over the internet.
5 It's unlikely that imperfect t-shirts ______ at the music festival.
6 Illegal copies of the artist's drawings ______.
7 A waterproof and fireproof product ______.
8 The fake gold necklaces ______.

11.2 INTERNET TALES

1 VOCABULARY: Degrees of truth

A **Circle the correct words to complete the sentences.**

1 If you don't tell the truth, you're being *dishonest / honest*.
2 When you tell a lie to stop someone from being hurt, you tell a *suspicious / white* lie.
3 If people believe stories about something that actually never happened, then they fell for a *hoax / misinformation*.
4 A story or statement that's not true but is often repeated, and believed by many to be true, is an urban *legend / fact*.
5 When something is not completely correct, it is *accurate / inaccurate*.
6 When something is not real, it is *false / biased*.
7 If people feel that they can trust you, they call you *controversial / trustworthy*.
8 When you make something seem more important than it really is, it has been *exaggerated /misleading*.
9 You're *misleading / suspicious* when something doesn't seem right.
10 When a story could be true but might be invented, it is a *rumor / white lie*.
11 Something is *controversial / misinformation* when it causes disagreement and discussion.
12 If you like or dislike a person based on personal opinions, you are *suspicious / biased*.
13 It's *misinformation / controversial* when information is wrong or intended to deceive.
14 If a reporter uses a photo that suggests something that is not true, then the photo is *inaccurate / misleading*.
15 When something is exact and correct, it's *exaggerated / accurate*.

2 GRAMMAR: Passives with modals and modal-like expressions; passive infinitives

A **Complete the sentences with *be* or *to be*.**

1 Misleading stories shouldn't ______*be*______ discussed on the news.
2 This new smartphone seems ____________ the best thing since sliced bread.
3 That type of news has ____________ stopped from reaching the students.
4 This story is a hoax and shouldn't ____________ believed.
5 She didn't expect ____________ given an award for her news stories.
6 This report needs ____________ done by this afternoon.
7 That type of work couldn't ____________ done by one person.
8 I didn't want ____________ thought of as a dishonest person, so I told the truth.

B **Complete the sentences with a modal or modal-like expression from the box. Use the correct verb tense.**

could	expect	have	must
~~need~~	seem	should	want

1 All news stories ___*need*___ to be checked.
2 They didn't ______ their story to spread as quickly as it did.
3 All the information ______ be collected and recorded first.
4 You ______ better listen to him or you'll be fired from your job.
5 We ______ be given directions for how to use this machine. It's complicated.
6 This ______ to be an important issue these days.
7 Future problems ______ be avoided if you address these issues now.
8 Jenna didn't ______ to be part of our team anymore.

C THINK CRITICALLY **What do you think spreads faster: facts or lies? Give reasons why.**

3 GRAMMAR AND VOCABULARY

A **Write a sentence using the prompts and a word in the box. Use the passive forms with modals or modal-like expressions.**

~~accurate~~	false	hoax	misleading	rumor	trustworthy

1 only / information / report / news channel
Only accurate information should be reported on a news channel.
2 story / tell / reporters
3 publish / stop / magazines
4 stories / research / source
5 information / check / report
6 dangerous / avoid / penalty

11.3 BELIEVE IT OR NOT …

1 LISTENING

A 11.01 UNDERSTAND IMPORTANT DETAILS **Listen to Chris and Adam talk about a possible hoax. Check (✓) the points people make to argue that the moon landing was fake.**

1 The American flag was waving, but there's no atmosphere on the moon. ☐
2 There isn't a big hole where the jet engine lifted off the moon. ☐
3 The moon reflects light from the sun. ☐
4 There were suspicious shadows and other light sources. ☐
5 Stars in the background cannot be seen when photographs were taken. ☐
6 The flag hangs completely limp in space when he steps away from it. ☐
7 The moon's atmosphere wouldn't have changed. ☐

B 11.01 **Listen to the conversation again. Complete the sentences with a number from the box.**

21	billions	hundred	seven	ten	thirty

1 I heard that ________ percent of Americans now believe that the United States never went to the moon.
2 People talked about the American flag that was planted on the moon on July ________, 1969.
3 The moon's atmosphere is something like ________ trillion times less dense than Earth's atmosphere.
4 There are ________ of stars in space.
5 The moon reflects about ________ percent of the light from the sun.
6 Over a ________ trustworthy scientists showed that this point, as well as the other points, were easily proven false.

2 CRITICAL THINKING

A THINK CRITICALLY **Which are more believable – the arguments for or against the moon landing? Give reasons why.**

____

____

____

3 SPEAKING

A **(Circle) the correct word and then write *B* (Belief), *S* (Some belief), or *D* (Disbelief) beside each expression.**

1 **A** By 2030, everyone will be able to scan using their eyes.
B There's no *(truth) / right* in that. D

2 **A** I love to watch scary movies.
B Really? I've never watched one in my entire life, *believe / like* it or not. ____

3 **A** Did you hear the story about the woman with three heads?
B You're so funny! *Tell / don't tell* me another one. ____

4 **A** Eating only green vegetables can actually reverse the signs of aging.
B Hmmm. I find that *easy / hard* to believe. ____

5 **A** So, that computer virus they warned us about was a hoax?
B Yes, I'm absolutely *positive / right* it was. ____

6 **A** Did you hear about the new drug that can cure all diseases?
B Yeah, *wrong / right*! ____

7 **A** She takes the subway to work every day because it's fast.
B That's partly *true / false*. But she also doesn't like the bus. ____

8 **A** This story says that he lost his fortune because he was careless.
B There's probably some *truth / belief* in that. ____

B **Express belief or disbelief about the rumors using the expressions from exercise 3A.**

1 Did you hear the rumor about spaghetti growing on trees?
I did. There's no truth to it. Spaghetti is not a fruit or a nut.

2 Did you hear the rumor about an asteroid destroying Earth next year?
____

3 Do you think that dogs will really be able to talk one day?
____

4 I heard a rumor that people might soon be able to live to 150.
____

5 Drones are being used to find people lost at sea, believe it or not.
____

6 Someone said that by 2030, there won't be any clean water left in the world.
____

11.4 CONVINCE ME

1 READING

A **Read the article about diamonds. How are "fake" diamonds different from "real" diamonds? How are they the same?**

REAL FAKE DIAMONDS

For centuries, diamonds have been a symbol of wealth, status, and love. They are the subject of legends, fairy tales, and Hollywood movies. We value diamonds for their beauty, of course, but mostly because they are rare and their number is finite.

The diamond in a ring today was formed millions of years ago. Deep inside the earth, under conditions of extreme heat and pressure, carbon was pressed and cooked into the hardest of minerals. Powerful eruptions – bigger than any current volcano could produce – brought them to the surface. The conditions necessary to create diamonds no longer exist naturally, but they can be simulated in a lab. Instead of millions of years, man-made diamonds can be created in about a month.

Chemically, man-made diamonds are exactly the same as natural diamonds: They are 100% carbon, formed by high heat and immense pressure. They look identical, too. Even professional jewelers have a hard time telling them apart. In fact, the only real difference is history. For some people, however, history matters. A natural diamond has flaws that make it imperfect but also unique. Man-made diamonds are "too perfect."

Man-made diamonds have advantages over natural ones, beyond their lower price (usually about 30% less). They are not politically controversial, like the so-called "blood diamonds" of the past. Best of all, man-made diamonds can be made to order. If you want a stone of a particular size and with a slight pink color, you don't have to search the world for it. Just tell the manufacturer when you place your order. In a few weeks, you'll have your own personalized real fake diamond.

B UNDERSTAND WORDS IN CONTEXT **Read the article again. Then underline the correct definitions of the words.**

1 beyond: *more than just / related to*
2 finite: *limited / unlimited*
3 flaw: *big difference / error or imperfection*
4 mineral: *a type of stone, like marble or coal / an element, like carbon or oxygen*
5 pressure: *space / force*
6 simulate: *to prove the accuracy of / to copy or recreate*

2 CRITICAL THINKING

A THINK CRITICALLY **Would you say that man-made diamonds are fake diamonds? Why or why not? Imagine you wanted to buy a piece of diamond jewelry today. Would you choose natural or man-made diamonds? Why? Give at least three reasons to explain your preference.**

3 WRITING

A **Read the review about a face product. Does it sound fake? Would you want to try it? Why or why not? Underline the language used to persuade.**

HOME • ABOUT • NEWS • BLOG • CONTACT SIGN IN

Jessica M ★★★★★

Although some might say that MIRACLE FACE CREAM, a new anti-aging wrinkle cream on the market, doesn't work, I've tried it and I look younger!

This miracle cream can take years off your face in just three days. When I used it the first day, I could already see the difference. It erased all my lines and wrinkles. It's like an instant facelift. The special formula will make your skin look brighter and smoother, and if you have dark spots, they'll be completely gone, too.

Who needs plastic surgery when you have this cream? And the best thing about this cream is that you only need a small amount to cover your entire face. It's the best thing since sliced bread!

I firmly believe that this cream will be a success because it works. It's not cheap, but it's really worth it! And according to the company who makes it, they have a few celebrities who support it, too. I feel if the word gets out about this magic cream, you won't be able to order it anytime soon.

I hope you get the same amazing results that I've had with MIRACLE FACE CREAM!

Jessica

Like Comment

B **USE PERSUASIVE LANGUAGE Read the review again. Choose a product below and write a review with a strong opening sentence that gives the opposite opinion first. Use persuasive language.**

hair thickener	nail polish	shampoo for dry hair
shaving cream	sunglasses	toothpaste whitener

CHECK AND REVIEW

Read the statements. Can you do these things?

UNIT 11	Mark the boxes. ☑ I can do it. ? I am not sure. **I can …**	If you are not sure, go back to these pages in the Student's Book.
VOCABULARY	☐ **describe fake goods.** ☐ **talk about untrue information.**	page 108 page 110
GRAMMAR	☐ **use passive forms.** ☐ **use passive with modals and modal-like expressions, and passive infinitives.**	page 109 page 111
LISTENING AND SPEAKING SKILLS	☐ **listen for specific information.** ☐ **express belief and disbelief.**	page 112 page 113
READING AND WRITING SKILLS	☐ **work out meaning from context.** ☐ **write a persuasive essay.**	page 114 page 115

UNIT 12 GOT WHAT IT TAKES?

12.1 PRACTICE MAKES PERFECT

1 VOCABULARY: Skill and performance

A **Complete the sentences with the words in the box.**

analytical	artistic	athletic	competent	~~determined~~
gifted	imaginative	intellectual	logical	musical
skilled	talented	technical	trained	

1 Sebastian was ___determined___ to finish his medical degree to become a doctor.
2 I like romantic or funny movies, nothing too ______________ . I don't want to think too hard.
3 He's very ______________ in the arts and will likely be famous one day.
4 Her ______________ abilities show in every soccer game.
5 If I had any ______________ ability, I'd make a painting for this wall.
6 It was the ______________ thing to do in order to save time and money.
7 Luciana is not a/an ______________ musician. She has just begun to play the guitar.
8 He hasn't shown himself to be very ______________ at his job.
9 You have a/an ______________ mind, so writing a story will be easy for you.
10 He has always been naturally ______________ , even from an early age.
11 She wasn't ______________ properly to do this type of job.
12 I wish I could sing, but I have no ______________ ability at all.
13 You need to have ______________ and ______________ skills if you want to be an engineer.

2 GRAMMAR: Adverbs with adjectives and adverbs

A **Underline the adverb that provides more detail about the adjective or adverb in the sentence. Circle the modified word and identify it as *Adj.* (Adjective) or *Adv.* (Adverb) next to each sentence.**

1 She became amazingly quick at solving math problems. ___Adj___
2 Some children are exceptionally bright. ______
3 I think she is really funny. ______
4 He picked up the baby extremely gently. ______
5 It'll sell especially well just by word of mouth. ______
6 Learning a new language never came particularly easily to me. ______
7 Can I be brutally honest with you? ______
8 Henry did a fairly good job on his English test. ______

B **Add more detail to each sentence by adding the adverb in parentheses.**

1 I thought she looked beautiful when she walked down the aisle. (amazingly)
I thought she looked amazingly beautiful when she walked down the aisle.

2 But it's not true. (necessarily)

3 It's supposed to be cloudy tomorrow. (partly)

4 I'm excited about going backstage after the concert. (especially)

5 They weren't interested in buying the house, but they said they'd think about it. (particularly)

6 There was enough food in the cupboards. (barely)

7 There's plenty of food leftover after dinner. (always)

8 He walked quickly down the street. (rather)

3 GRAMMAR AND VOCABULARY

A **Write sentences using your own ideas and the word prompts.**

1 exceptionally / athletic
She's exceptionally athletic when it comes to sports .

2 amazingly / intellectual
.

3 especially / logical
.

4 hardly / trained
.

5 extremely / gifted
.

6 particularly / musical
.

B **Complete the sentences so that they are true for you. Use an adverb to modify the adjectives.**

1 I think I'm skilled at ______ .
2 I don't think I'm imaginative when it comes to ______ .
3 I'm competent at ______ .
4 When I was younger, I was talented at ______ .
5 I'm determined to ______ .

12.2 CHANGE THE WORLD

1 VOCABULARY: Describing emotional impact

A **Circle the correct word(s) in each sentence.**

1 He tried to *raise her spirits / ruin her day* by taking her out to a fancy restaurant.
2 All this extra work is going to *make my day / stress me out.*
3 I need to *take my mind off of this matter / raise somebody's spirits* for a while and just relax.
4 Taking a vacation right now might *make your day / do you good.*
5 The books he writes *capture the imagination of children / are a real downer* all over the world.
6 He *brightens up / gets down* just thinking about his boring job.
7 She *ruined my day / put my mind at rest* when she walked away without apologizing.
8 The memory of this vacation will *do me good / leave a lasting impression on me.*
9 Finding $10 on the bus today really *took my mind off / brightened up* my day.
10 Rainy days can *stress me out / be a real downer.* They make everything look so gray.
11 It *captured her imagination / made her day* when her best friend called.
12 Once you know the reason, you can relax and *brighten up / put your mind at rest.*

B **Complete the sentences using phrases from exercise 1A . More than one answer can be correct for some sentences.**

1 When my friend is down, I ___brighten up___ her day with some chocolate ice cream.
2 Traffic in the morning can really ______________ when I'm trying to get to work on time.
3 Taking the afternoon off to enjoy the sunny weather might ______________ .
4 Seeing him cry can ______________ for me.
5 Knowing Adam was safe at home ______________ .
6 Her incredible story has ______________ .
7 I need to leave the office for a while and ______________ work.
8 The flowers he sent ______________ .

2 GRAMMAR: Making non-count nouns countable

A **Complete the sentences with an expression in the box.**

a bunch of	~~a cup of~~	a piece of	a slice of	piece of	work of

1 Do you want to have ___a cup of___ tea before you go?
2 She had ______________ lemon pie for dessert.
3 This sculpture is a real ______________ art.
4 I listened to a wonderful ______________ music when I was at her house.
5 She bought ______________ stuff at the store.
6 My professor gave me ______________ advice about my future goals.

B **Correct the mistake(s) in each sentence. Then underline the expression that makes the non-count noun countable.**

1 Everyone should show a little bit~~s~~ of kindness to their neighbors.

2 I heard a great pieces of advice on the radio today.

3 I had a slice of cake and two cup of coffee for lunch today.

4 There was a bunches of newspaper on the table.

5 Ariana and her friends played a games of cards at the party.

6 Would you like a slices of cheese on your hamburger?

7 Can I have two piece of bread with my dinner?

3 GRAMMAR AND VOCABULARY

A **Write sentences using your own ideas and the word prompts. Make the non-count nouns countable.**

1 coffee / brighten up sth

He brightened up my day when he bought me a cup of coffee .

2 music / capture sb's imagination

____.

3 kindness / make sb's day

____.

4 advice / raise sb's spirits

____.

5 chess / take sb's mind off sth

____.

6 art / leave a lasting impression on sb

____.

7 cake / do sb good

____.

B **THINK CRITICALLY** **In your opinion, what are some things we could do to make someone's day positive? What are some things that might make someone's day negative?**

12.3 MAYBE ONE DAY ...

1 LISTENING

A 12.01 **Listen to the conversation. Match each statement.**

1 Work *d*
2 Develop ____
3 There are many websites that ____
4 There are a lot of workshops ____
5 Write for ____
6 Enjoy it and ____

a can teach you how to write.
b the love of it.
c technical skills.
d hard.
e you'll be successful at it.
f you can take.

B 12.01 LISTEN FOR CONTRASTING IDEAS **Listen to the conversation again. Are the ideas optimistic or cautious? Write *O* or *C* next to each one.**

1 I can't say for certain that all these imaginative stories in my head will turn into books. *C*
2 But I'm confident that one day it'll happen. ____
3 I saw no reason why I couldn't. ____
4 There was no guarantee that it would happen. ____
5 There's no harm in trying to learn how to write. ____
6 Well, things might not go as planned. ____

2 CRITICAL THINKING

A THINK CRITICALLY **Do you think Valeria has the right attitude to become a famous author? Why or why not?**

3 SPEAKING

A **Complete the expressions with a word from the box. Then put them in the correct columns.**

certain	confident	guarantee	harm	planned	~~reason~~

1 I see no *reason* why (I can't).
2 I can't say for ______.
3 I will do this. I'm ______ that …
4 I realize that things might not go as ______.
5 There's no ______ in trying.
6 There's no ______ that …

Expressing optimism	Expressing caution
I see no reason why (I can't.)	

B **For each situation, complete responses to express both optimism and caution. Use expressions from 3A.**

1 Can you help me move some boxes this weekend?
A *I see no reason why I can't. I'm not working* .
B *I can't say for certain, but I might be working* .
2 I'd love to travel there one day.
A ______.
B ______.
3 My dream scenario would be to have my own business.
A ______.
B ______.
4 Can we try to get tickets to the game on Saturday?
A ______.
B ______.
5 My ultimate goal next year is to become a music teacher at this school.
A ______.
B ______.

12.4 SUCCESS BEHIND THE SCENES

1 READING

A **Do you think working as an actress is fun and exciting? Read the article. Was your prediction correct? What was the day like for the actress?**

Life as an actress

By Mariel van White

Yesterday, I had the opportunity to spend the day with an amazingly talented actress, Ashley Stone. And from what I experienced, being an actress not only takes a lot of skill, but determination and patience, too.

As soon as she arrived to work, at 6.00 a.m., she got checked for hair, makeup, and wardrobe. These things need to be perfect when the camera is rolling. After that, she checked in with the assistant director to make sure there hadn't been any changes to her lines. There had—and it seems there are script changes most days—so she had to memorize them before she was called in front of the cameras.

When Ashley got to the set, the director and crew were busy setting up the scene with special lights and checking camera angles. She stood around waiting, and waiting … and then, when it was time to step in front of the cameras, someone had to adjust her makeup while the wardrobe assistant checked her outfit, again!

After an *exceptionally* long time, she got to say her lines. But right in the middle of them, the director shouted "Cut!" Something wasn't perfect. It was a missing light. There are little problems like this all the time on a movie set. Ashley just had to go back to her trailer to practice her lines again. When all the actors were called back to the set, the scene was shot before another break, this time for lunch. After lunch, Ashley and the other actors spent the rest of the day shooting scenes and rehearsing for the next day. Finally, but not until 10.00 p.m., someone called it a wrap—time for everyone to go home.

Fun? It certainly didn't seem like it. There was a lot of standing around. You need to be extremely focused and patient. That's part of what acting is all about. But Ashley told me it's worth it in the end because when the film is released, millions of people around the world will see her work on the big screen.

B **UNDERSTAND CAUSE AND EFFECT** **Read again. What is/was the result of each of these events?**

1 The actress arrived to work.
2 The assistant director changed the lines.
3 There was a missing light.
4 Actors were called back to the set.
5 Someone called it a wrap.
6 The film is released.

2 CRITICAL THINKING

A **THINK CRITICALLY** **Make a list of some other jobs that might seem exciting and fascinating, like an actor's. Choose one and think about what the reality of the job might be like.**

3 WRITING

A **Read Amelia's review of a movie. Did she like it? Why or why not? Underline words that show reasons or results.**

Reply Forward

To: Christian
From: Amelia
Subject: Favorite Movies

Hi Christian,

I just got back from seeing the sequel to *After the Attack*. I know the first one was one of your favorite movies. But this one was really bad, so don't waste your time!

The special effects were done exceptionally well, but the dialogue and plot were too simple. It felt like it was made for kids, so I got bored halfway through. The acting was OK, but because of the unknown actors, I wasn't connecting to anyone. There was some beautiful scenery which was as impressive as the special effects, but nothing like the first movie. The scenes were too long and drawn out; consequently, I fell into a deep sleep.

Anyway, I thought I'd save you some money!

Can't wait to see you this weekend!

Amelia

B **SHOW REASON AND RESULT** **Think about a movie you liked or didn't like. Write a review of it using words such as *so, therefore, as a result,* and *consequently.***

CHECK AND REVIEW

Read the statements. Can you do these things?

UNIT 12	Mark the boxes. ☑ I can do it. ? I am not sure. **I can ...**	If you are not sure, go back to these pages in the Student's Book.
VOCABULARY	☐ **talk about talents and skills.** ☐ **describe how to make life better.**	page 118 page 120
GRAMMAR	☐ **use adverbs with adjectives and adverbs.** ☐ **make non-count nouns countable.**	page 119 page 121
LISTENING AND SPEAKING SKILLS	☐ **describe your ambitions.** ☐ **express optimistic and cautious opinions.**	page 122 page 123
READING AND WRITING SKILLS	☐ **understand cause and effect.** ☐ **write a review of a performance.**	page 124 page 125

1.5 TIME TO SPEAK A step forward

A **Talk to someone you know who is a generation or more older than you (parent, grandparent, teacher, etc.). Try to speak in English, if possible. Take notes in English. Use the questions below to help you.**

- Ask how life was different in the past compared to the present.
- Ask about any new technology he or she witnessed, the type of clothes he or she wore, the different kinds of entertainment, what school was like, and so on.

B **During your next class, discuss your results with a classmate.**

2.5 TIME TO SPEAK Natural limits

A **Search online for outdoor adventure travel companies. Look at a few different websites and identify an outdoor adventure you are interested in. Write down at least three questions you have about your selected trip and research the answers.**

B **Tell a classmate about your activity. Did you have the same questions? How are your activities similar?**

3.5 TIME TO SPEAK The way I am

A **Interview someone who has an interesting job. Interview the person in English, if possible. Take notes. Use the prompts below to help you.**

- Ask the person to describe the job.
- Then ask what qualities a person should have in order to do the job well.

B **During your next class, share your findings with a classmate.**

4.5 TIME TO SPEAK It takes a team

A **Think of or research a list of jobs you could do from home. Write the advantages and disadvantages of working from home.**

Jobs you can do from home	Advantages	Disadvantages

B **Present your ideas in your next class. Compare your ideas with other students.**

5.5 TIME TO SPEAK The human factor

A **Create a survey about cell phone behavior. Think of four or five questions to ask. Give the survey to your family and friends. Use the example questions below to help you.**

Example survey questions

- Do you think it's OK to eat while you're talking on your cell phone?
- What annoys you the most about other people's cell phone behavior?
- Do you use your cell phone when you're in a restaurant? Why or why not?

B **Bring the results to your next class and share them with your classmates. Who had the most interesting survey questions and responses?**

6.5 TIME TO SPEAK Expect the unexpected

A **Prepare to tell a story about one of the topics below. Make some notes. Practice telling your story by saying it out loud. You can also record yourself and listen to your story to see if you want to make any changes.**

Topics:

- the worst haircut I ever received
- the first/last day at my job or at school
- a time when I miscommunicated with someone

B **Tell your story to a friend, family member, or classmate. Ask them if they have a story about a similar topic.**

7.5 TIME TO SPEAK Negotiate for a price

A **Look for three to five items in your home that you no longer want. Answer the questions below for each item.**

- What makes the item worth selling?
- What would be the highest price you would want to get for it?
- What would be the lowest price you would sell it for?

B **Take your list of items to your next class. Bring photos of the items if you can. Negotiate and bargain for a price for other items in the classroom and for the items you are selling.**

8.5 TIME TO SPEAK Make a podcast on ways to reduce stress

A **Think of the last time you were really stressed. Make notes. Use the questions below to help you.**

- What were you stressed about?
- What action or actions did you take to reduce the stress?
- Was this action simple and effective?

B **Share what happened and what you did in your next class.**

9.5 TIME TO SPEAK Talk about key events in your life

A **Think of important or interesting things you've done or experienced in the past five years. Use the questions below to help you.**

- What have I done or experienced?
- What have I been doing in my free time?
- Do I have any regrets?
- Have my relationships been good or bad?
- Where have I traveled/worked?

B **Share your list and then listen to a partner's list. Make positive comments about good things you hear and reassuring comments about not-so-good things.**

10.5 TIME TO SPEAK Attracting talent

A **Go online and find three companies where experienced and talented employees would want to work. Use the questions below to help you.**

- Who are they?
- What do they do?
- Why would employees like to work for them?
- What makes their websites attractive?

B **Create a presentation about your companies and bring it to your next class. What company would your class like to work for the most? What about the least? Ask the class to give you reasons.**

11.5 TIME TO SPEAK Does it really work?

A **Think of a tip that you might follow when you are sick with a cold or flu. Use the questions below to help you.**

- What is the tip?
- Where did you find it?
- What do you have to do?
- How effective is it?

B **In your next class, present your tip to the class. As a class, choose the tips you believe will be the most effective.**

12.5 TIME TO SPEAK Me, in two minutes

A **Go online and research someone famous with a special talent. Use the questions below to help you.**

- What skills does/did the person have?
- Was the person born gifted or trained?
- What has the person done?

B **In your next class, pretend you are this person. Describe your talents and abilities for about two minutes to the class. The class then asks questions to find out who you are.**

NOTES

The authors and publishers acknowledge the following sources of copyright material and are grateful for the permissions granted. While every effort has been made, it has not always been possible to identify the sources of all the material used, or to trace all copyright holders. If any omissions are brought to our notice, we will be happy to include the appropriate acknowledgments on reprinting & in the next update to the digital edition, as applicable.

Key: U = Unit.

Text
U9: Daniel Wendler for the adapted text from 'The Secret Of Conversation Flow', https://www.improveyoursocialskills.com/conversation/conversation-flow. Copyright © Daniel Wendler. Reproduced with kind permission. **U10**: The Professional Writer for the adapted text from 'How to write a Company Profile that wins business' by LYNDALL. Copyright © The Professional Writer. Reproduced with kind permission of Lyndall Guinery-Smith.

Photographs
The following photographs are sourced from Getty Images.

U1: Absodels/ABSODELS/Getty Images Plus; Alistair Berg/DigitalVision; Cavan Images/Cavan; Chris Tobin/DigitalVision; Steve Debenport/E+; Hemant Mehta; Schon & Probst/Picture Press/Getty Images Plus; **U2:** Stocktrek Images; Monty Rakusen/Cultura; Rohit Singh/EyeEm; Photography by Thy Bun/Moment Open; Stuart Westmorland/Corbis Documentary/Getty Images Plus; shalamov/iStock/Getty Images Plus; A. Martin UW Photography/Moment; Rob Janné/500px Prime; Westend61; **U3:** Dougal Waters/DigitalVision; Carlina Teteris/Moment; Caiaimage/Lukas Olek; -goldy-/iStock/Getty Images Plus; monkeybusinessimages/iStock/Getty Images Plus; Tomas Rodriguez/Corbis; Tom Kelley Archive/Retrofile RF; **U4:** Maskot; LightFieldStudios/iStock/Getty Images Plus; shapecharge/E+; Caiaimage/Paul Bradbury; Hoxton/Tom Merton; skynesher/E+; portishead1/E+; Hero Images/DigitalVision; **U5:** GSPictures/E+; Westend61; Compassionate Eye Foundation/Dan Kenyon/DigitalVision; Hero Images; Sasha Bell/Moment; Caiaimage/Paul Bradbury; **U6:** Jupiterimages/Stockbyte; oberschneider/RooM; Fancy/Veer/Corbis; Westend61; Hero Images; Hero Images; David Oliver/Taxi/Getty Images Plus; Fresh photos from all over the worls/Moment; **U7:** Westend61; LenaSkor/iStock/Getty Images Plus; blue jean images; Anfisa Kameneva/EyeEm; claudio.arnese/E+; Maskot; Tim Robberts/Taxi/Getty Images Plus; **U8:** Kathleen Finlay/Image Source; Westend61; skynesher/E+; FangXiaNuo/E+; WHL; **U9:** sturti/E+; Neustockimages/E+; Deagreez/iStock/Getty Images Plus; Maskot; bernardbodo/iStock/Getty Images Plus; **U10:** Eugenio Marongiu/Cultura; Hero Images; PeopleImages/E+; F.J. Jiménez/Moment; MangoStar_Studio/iStock/Getty Images Plus; mustafagull/E+; Petardj/iStock/Getty Images Plus; John Harper/Moment; levente bodo/Moment; pixelfit/E+; skynesher/E+; gradyreese/E+; **U11:** JAY DIRECTO/AFP; mustafagull/E+; Strauss/Curtis; Mihajlo Maricic/EyeEm; World Perspectives/Photographer's Choice/Getty Images Plus; Photographer is my life/Moment; mevans/E+; **U12:** andresr/E+; Michael Blann/DigitalVision; Hinterhaus Productions/Taxi/Getty Images Plus; Chaiyaporn Baokaew/Moment; Westend61; Paolo Sartori; Yurdakul/E+.

Front cover photography by Hans Neleman/The Image Bank/Getty Images Plus/Getty Images.

Typeset by emc design ltd.

Audio
Audio production by CityVox, New York.

URL
The publisher has used its best endeavors to ensure that the URLs for external websites referred to in this book are correct and active at the time of going to press. However, the publisher has no responsibility for the websites and can make no guarantee that a site will remain live or that the content is or will remain appropriate.

Corpus
Development of this publication has made use of the Cambridge English Corpus (CEC). The CEC is a multi-billion word collection of contemporary spoken and written English. It includes British English, American English, and other varieties. It also includes the Cambridge Learner Corpus, the world's biggest collection of learner writing, developed in collaboration with Cambridge Assessment. Cambridge University Press uses the CEC to provide evidence about language use that helps to produce better language teaching materials. Our Evolve authors study the Corpus to see how English is really used, and to identify typical learner mistakes. This information informs the authors' selection of vocabulary, grammar items and Student's Book Corpus features such as the Accuracy Check, Register Check, and Insider English.